J. D. VANCE

Biography

Hillbilly Elegy and the Man It Created

TABLE OF CONTENTS

CHAPTER 1

I learnt my home address, like most young children, so that I could tell an adult where to take me if I got lost. Even though my mother changed addresses a lot for reasons I didn't understand as a child, I was able to recall the address without missing a beat when the kindergarten teacher asked me where I lived. Nevertheless, I always made a distinction between "my address" and "my home." I spent most of my time with my mother and sister, wherever they could be, at my residence. However, my home—my great-grandmother's house in the holler in Jackson, Kentucky—never changed.

Located in the coal belt of southeast Kentucky, Jackson is a small town of roughly 6,000 residents. To refer to it as a town is rather altruistic: A courthouse, a few eateries (almost all fast-food franchises), and a few more shops and retailers are all there. The majority of the population resides in trailer parks, government-subsidized housing, modest farmhouses, mountain homesteads like the one that provided the setting for my favorite childhood memories, and the mountains surrounding Kentucky Highway 15.

Every time a funeral parade passes by, Jacksonians greet everyone, voluntarily forego their favorite activities to dig a stranger's car out of the snow, and, without fail, stop their cars, get out, and stand at attention. I became aware of something unique about Jackson and its inhabitants because of that latter practice. Why did everyone pause for the passing hearse, I would ask my grandmother, whom we all called Mamaw. "Because we're hill people, honey." We also honor our deceased.

I grew up in Middletown, Ohio, where my grandparents raised their family after leaving Jackson in the late 1940s. However, I spent most of my remaining years and my summers back in Jackson until I was twelve. Mamaw, who was always aware that time was reducing the number of her favorite people, would bring me along when she wanted to see friends and family. As time passed, we traveled primarily to care for Mamaw's mother, whom we referred to as Mamaw Blanton (to differentiate her from Mamaw, though this was a little confusing). Mamaw Blanton hosted us in the home she had occupied since before her husband departed to fight the Japanese in the Pacific.

Despite not being big or opulent, Mamaw Blanton's house was my favorite spot on earth. There were three bedrooms in the house. It had a big yard that extended to the head of the holler on one side and into a mountain on the other, and a modest porch with a porch swing. Mamaw Blanton had some land, but it was mostly inhospitable vegetation. There was a lovely mountaintop of granite and trees, but no backyard to brag about. That was enough for the backyard. There was always the holler and the creek that flowed beside it. All of the children shared a single room upstairs, a squad cell with perhaps a dozen beds, where my cousins and I would play until our agitated grandmother scared us into sleep.

I spent most of my time frightening the Appalachian wildlife—no turtle, snake, frog, fish, or squirrel was safe—because the surrounding mountains were a child's heaven. Unaware of Mamaw Blanton's failing health or the constant poverty, I would run about with my cousins.

Deep down, Mamaw, my sister, and I all felt that Jackson was our place. Although I had many unpleasant recollections of Ohio, I still liked it. In Ohio, I was the abandoned son of a man I hardly knew and a mother I wished I didn't know; in Jackson, I was the grandson of the most talented auto mechanic in town and the fiercest woman anybody knew. Mamaw made sure to bring no drama to Mom's visits to Kentucky, which were limited to the yearly family reunion and the occasional funeral. There would be no yelling, no fighting, no beatings of my sister. Most importantly, Mamaw would remark, "no men," in Jackson. Mamaw disapproved of all of Mom's romantic partners and forbade them from entering Kentucky.

I had been particularly adept at dealing with different parent figures in Ohio. I feigned that earrings were cool with Steve, a midlife crisis sufferer who had an earring to prove it, to the point where he felt it was appropriate to pierce my ear as well. I adored police cars and had thick skin with Chip, an alcoholic cop who thought my earring was a sign of "girlieness." I was a loving brother to his two kids with Ken, a strange guy who asked Mom to marry him three days into their relationship. However, none of these claims were accurate. I knew that by the following year, Ken's kids would no longer be in my life, and I detested police cars and earrings. The only guys in my life, my grandmother's brothers and brothers-in-law, already knew me, so I didn't have to try to be someone I wasn't in Kentucky. Was it my intention to make them proud? Of course I did, but I truly loved them, not just because I feigned liking them.

Uncle Teaberry, who got his moniker from his favorite chewing gum flavor, was the eldest and cruelest of the Blanton men. During World War II, Uncle Teaberry served in the navy, like his father. I only have two genuine recollections of dad because he passed away when I was four years old. In the first, Teaberry is right behind me with a switchblade, promising to feed my right ear to the dogs if he gets me while I'm running for my life. After I jump into Mamaw Blanton's embrace, the frightful game is finished. However, I am certain that I loved him since my second recollection is of being so upset about not being able to see him while he was dying that my grandmother had to put on a medical robe and sneak me in. I don't recall saying goodbye, but I do recall holding on to her under that hospital gown.

Uncle Pet followed. Uncle Pet was a tall man with a bawdy sense of humor and a sharp wit. Uncle Pet, the Blanton crew's most prosperous member, left home early and began a few construction and lumbering enterprises that earned him enough cash to engage in horse racing during his free time. He had the easy charm of a prosperous businessman and appeared to be the kindest of the Blanton men. However, that appeal concealed a fiery temper. A truck driver once said to my old hillbilly uncle, "Off-load this now, you son of a bitch," after delivering supplies to one of Uncle Pet's enterprises. "When you say that, you're calling my dear old mother a bitch, so I'd kindly ask you to speak more carefully," Uncle Pet said, taking the remark literally. Uncle Pet did what any sensible business owner would do when the driver, known as Big Red due to his size and hair color, continued to insult him: he dragged the man out of his truck, beat him unconscious, and slashed his body with an electric saw. Big Red almost died from bleeding, but he was taken to the hospital and lived. But Uncle Pet never ended up behind bars. Big Red was reportedly also an Appalachian man. He declined to report the incident to the authorities or file a report. He was aware of the consequences of insulting a man's mother.

Of Mamaw's brothers, Uncle David might have been the only one who didn't give a damn about that honor culture. He enjoyed everything but regulations, which may be why he didn't try to justify his enormous marijuana plant when I discovered it in the rear of the former homestead. He was an elderly rebel with long, flowing hair and a larger beard. Startled, I inquired about Uncle David's intentions about illegal substances. He then got a lighter and some cigarette papers and showed them to me. I was twelve. I knew Mamaw would kill him if she ever found out.

Mamaw had almost killed a guy, according to family legend, therefore I was afraid of this. Two men were loading the family's cow—a valuable asset in a society without running water—into the back of a truck when Mamaw, who was about twelve at the time, went outside. She sprinted inside, snatched up a rifle, and shot a couple of shots. A shot to the leg caused one of the men to collapse, while the other leaped into the vehicle and screeched out of it. Since the would-be robber was scarcely able to walk, Mamaw went up to him, held her rifle's business end up to his head, and got ready to complete the task. Fortunately for him, Uncle Pet stepped in. It would have to wait till another day for Mamaw to have her first confirmed kill.

I find this story hard to believe, even considering how crazy Mamaw was about carrying a pistol. About half of my family members had never heard the story, according to a survey I conducted. I think if someone had not intervened, she would have killed the man. Class betrayal was the worst kind of disloyalty, and she detested it. Like a general giving his troops marching orders, Mom would tell me, "There is nothing lower than the poor stealing from the poor," if someone stole a bike from our porch (three times, by my count), broke into her car and took the spare change, or stole a delivery. It's already difficult enough. We really don't need to make things harder for each other.

Uncle Gary was the youngest of the Blanton boys. He was one of the sweetest men I had ever met and the family's baby. Uncle Gary established a prosperous roofing company in Indiana after leaving home at an early age. He was a wonderful husband and father, and whenever he told me, "We're proud of you, ole Jaydot," I felt a surge of pride. The only Blanton brother who didn't threaten me with a boot to the ass or a cold ear, he was my favorite.

Although I adored both of my grandma's younger sisters, Betty and Rose, I was completely enamored with the Blanton males. I would sit with them and ask them to share their stories again and again. I was the best student of these guys, who guarded the family's oral legacy.

The majority of this custom was definitely not suitable for children. For the most part, it was the kind of brutality that should get someone jailed. A lot of it focused on how Breathitt, the county where Jackson lived, came to be known by the alliterative moniker "Bloody Breathitt." There were numerous answers, but they all had the same idea: Breathitt residents didn't need the legislation to suppress their hatred.

The story of the older man in town who was accused of raping a little girl was one of the most popular stories of Breathitt's gore. Mamaw informed me that the man was discovered facedown in a nearby lake with sixteen gunshot wounds to his back just days prior to his trial. The murder was never investigated by authorities, and the local newspaper only mentioned it the morning his body was found. A man was discovered dead, the publication stated in a commendable display of journalistic wit. Expect foul play. I would hear my grandmother yell, "Is foul play expected?" "You're absolutely correct. That son of a bitch was reached by Bloody Breathitt.

Uncle Teaberry also remembered the day he heard a young man mention wanting to "eat her panties," a reference to his sister's (my Mamaw's) underwear. After driving home, Uncle Teaberry took out Mamaw's panties and made the young man eat them at knifepoint.

Some folks could think that I'm from a crazy clan. However, because my people were on the right side of these traditional good-versus-evil tales, I felt like hillbilly royalty. My folks were severe, but only when it served a purpose, like protecting a sister's dignity or making sure a criminal was held accountable for his misdeeds. The Blanton guys, such as the tomboy Blanton sister I nicknamed Mamaw enforced hillbilly justice, and I thought it was the best kind of justice.

The Blanton men were rife with vice, either in spite of or perhaps because of their virtues. Some of them left wives who were unfaithful, neglected children, or both. Furthermore, I only saw them on the holidays or at big family gatherings, so I didn't really know them well. I still worshipped and adored them. A lot of father figures had come and gone, but the Blanton men were always there, so I once heard Mamaw tell her mother that I adored them. There is definitely some truth. Above all, however, the Blanton men were the living embodiment of Kentucky's hills. Because I adored Jackson, I also loved them.

My fascination with the Blanton guys subsided into admiration as I got older, and my perception of Jackson as a kind of utopia also changed. Jackson will always feel like home to me. It's unbelievably gorgeous: Every mountain in town appears to be on fire when the leaves change in October. For all its charm and happy memories, Jackson is a really cruel place. I learned from Jackson that "poor people" and "hill people" typically meant the same thing. We would have fried bologna sandwiches for lunch, soup beans and cornbread for dinner, then scrambled eggs, ham, fried potatoes, and biscuits for breakfast at Mamaw Blanton's. As I became older, I heard the grownups talk about the pathetic, malnourished children in the neighborhood and how the town should aid them, which made me aware that many Jackson families couldn't say the same. Mamaw protected me from Jackson's worst side, but you can only ignore reality for so long.

I made sure to visit Mamaw Blanton's former home, which is currently occupied by my second cousin Rick and his family, during a recent trip to Jackson. We discussed the changes that had occurred. Rick informed me, "Drugs have come in." "And no one is eager to continue working." I requested Rick's lads to accompany me for a walk since I hoped my beloved Holler had survived the worst. I observed the most severe manifestations of Appalachian poverty everywhere.

Some of it was as cliché as it was heartbreaking: old furniture scattered over the lawns, shabby shacks decaying away, and stray dogs pleading for food. Some of it was much more. I saw a terrified pair of eyes peering at me from behind the curtains of a bedroom window as I passed a modest two-bedroom house. I was intrigued, so I took a closer look and saw that there were eight different sets of eyes watching me from three windows with a startling mix of love and dread. A slender man, perhaps no more than thirty-five, who appeared to be the leader of the house, stood on the front porch. The furniture scattered over the empty front yard was guarded by a number of vicious, emaciated, chained dogs. Rick's son told me that the young father had no job and was proud of it when I asked him what he did for a living. However, he continued, "we just try to avoid them because they're mean."

Although this house may be extravagant, it reflects a lot of Jackson's hill people's life. About half of Jackson's youngsters are among the nearly one-third of the town's population that live in poverty. The vast majority of Jacksonians live below the poverty line, and that doesn't include them. Prescription medication abuse has spread like wildfire. The state of Kentucky recently took control of the public schools because they are so awful. Despite this, parents send their kids to these schools since they don't have much extra cash, and the high school consistently fails to send its students to college. The population is physically ill, and they are unable to receive treatment for even the most basic issues without government support. Above all, they are cruel about it. They will be reluctant to share details of their lives with others for the straightforward reason that they do not want to be evaluated.

A 2009 ABC News story about Appalachian America focused on a condition called locally as "Mountain Dew mouth," which is characterized by excruciating dental issues in young children that are typically brought on by consuming excessive amounts of sugary soda. ABC's presentation included a long list of accounts of Appalachian youngsters who were facing deprivation and poverty. Despite being extensively viewed in the area, the news report was completely derided. This is none of your dang concern, is the standard response. One online commentator stated, "This has to be the most offensive thing I have ever heard and you should all be ashamed, ABC included." Another said, "You should feel ashamed of yourself for perpetuating outdated, untrue stereotypes and failing to present a more truthful image of Appalachia." I have met many people in real alpine rural villages who share this viewpoint.

I was aware of this because my cousin used Facebook to silence the critics, stating that the only way for people to hope to address the region's problems was to acknowledge them. Amber is in a unique position to discuss Appalachia's issues: She was born and raised in Jackson, unlike me. She excelled academically in high school and became the first person in her immediate family to receive a college degree. She personally saw the worst of Jackson's poverty and managed to overcome it.

The outraged response backs up the scholarly research on Appalachian Americans. Sociologists Carol A. Markstrom, Sheila K. Marshall, and Robin J. Tryon discovered in a December 2000 study that avoidance and wishful-thinking coping strategies "significantly predicted resiliency" in Appalachian teenagers. According to their study, hillbillies are taught to cope with unpleasant realities by denying them or by acting as though there are better realities. Although this inclination may contribute to psychological resilience, it also makes it difficult for Appalachians to examine themselves objectively.

We have a tendency to exaggerate and understate, to emphasize our virtues while ignoring our flaws. For this reason, an honest look at some of Appalachia's poorest residents sparked a significant reaction from the region's residents. That's why I idolized the Blanton guys and pretended that everything in the world was wrong except for me for the first eighteen years of my life.

The truth is difficult, and for hill people, the facts they have to face about themselves are the most difficult. Unquestionably, Jackson is home to some of the kindest people on the planet, but it is also home to drug addicts and at least one father who manages to have eight children but is unable to provide for them. Unquestionably, it is gorgeous, but the loose trash and environmental debris that litter the landscape overshadow its beauty. With the obvious exception of the large number of food stamp beneficiaries who have no interest in honest labor, its citizens are hardworking. Jackson is inconsistent, as are Blanton guys.

Things have gotten so terrible that my cousin Mike's first instinct after burying his mother last summer was to sell her house. He declared, "I can't live here, and I can't neglect it." "The drug users will loot it." Although Jackson has always been impoverished, men there have never been afraid to leave their mothers' house by themselves. My hometown has taken a troubling turn.

If one is tempted to dismiss these issues as the exclusive domain of rural hollers, a look at my own life shows that Jackson's predicament has gained widespread attention. Hillbilly values and hillbilly people spread extensively due to the large-scale migration from Appalachia's poorest areas to states like Ohio, Michigan, Indiana, Pennsylvania, and Illinois. In fact, Middletown, Ohio, where I grew up, is so populated by Kentucky transplants and their offspring that we used to mock it as "Middletucky."

In some respects, my grandparents found a better life in Middletucky after leaving the real Kentucky and moving there. They never truly escaped in other respects. Their oldest daughter has suffered from Jackson's drug addiction throughout her adult life. Although Mountain

Dew mouth is particularly acute in Jackson, my grandparents also battled it in Middletown: Mamaw first noticed my mother pouring Pepsi into my bottle when I was nine months old. In Jackson, there aren't many good fathers, but my grandparents' grandchildren also don't have many. For decades, people have been fighting to leave Jackson; now, they are fighting to leave Middletown.

It's unclear exactly where the issues stop if they begin in Jackson. Observing that funeral procession with Mamaw many years ago let me know that I am a hill person. So is much of the white working class in America. And things aren't going well for us hill people.

Chapter 2

Hillbillies enjoy putting their own spin on many words. We refer to crayfish as "crawdads" and minnows as "miners." The definition of "hollow" is a "valley or basin," but I've never used the term until I had to clarify for a buddy what I meant when I said "holler." Other people call their grandparents a variety of names, including grannie, pop-pop, nanna, and grandpa. However, outside of our community, I've never heard someone use "Mamaw," which is pronounced ma'am-aw, or "Papaw." Only hillbilly grandparents have these names.

Without a doubt or reservation, my grandparents, Mamaw and Papaw, were the best things that ever happened to me. They taught me the life lessons that most people learn from their parents and spent the last 20 years of their lives demonstrating to me the importance of stability and love. Both contributed to giving me the opportunities and self-assurance I needed to have a fair chance at the American Dream. However, I don't think Bonnie Blanton and Jim Vance had high expectations for their own lives as kids. How were they able to? Big ideas are rarely fostered by single-room, K–12 schoolhouses and the Appalachian hills.

Papaw's early years are not well known to us, and I don't think that will ever change. We are aware that he was a member of the hillbilly nobility. Jim Vance, Papaw's distant cousin, married into the Hatfield family and became a member of the Wildcats, a group of ex-Confederate soldiers and supporters. One of the best-known family feuds in American history began when Cousin Jim killed Asa Harmon McCoy, a former Union soldier.

In 1929, Papaw was given the middle name James Lee Vance in honor of his father, Lee Vance. Papaw's overburdened mother, Goldie, sent him to live with her father, Pap Taulbee, a stern man who owned a small timber company, after Lee passed away a few months after Papaw was born. Goldie rarely saw her young son, but she did occasionally send money. Papaw would spend the first seventeen years of his life in Jackson, Kentucky, living with Taulbee.

The Blantons—Blaine and Hattie and their eight children—lived only a few hundred yards away from Pap Taulbee's small two-room home. Hattie became my grandfather's surrogate mother after feeling sorry for the little, motherless youngster. Jim quickly became an unnecessary family. He ate most of his meals in Hattie's kitchen and spent most of his free time playing with the Blanton boys. His ultimate marriage to her eldest daughter was inevitable.

Jim married into a boisterous group. In Breathitt, the Blantons were a well-known family with a rivalry history almost as storied as Papaw's. At the start of the twentieth century, Mamaw's great-grandfather had been elected county judge, but only after her grandfather, Tilden, the judge's son, murdered a member of a competing family on election day. Two things stand out in a piece on the violent feud in the New York Times. First, Tilden was never imprisoned for the offense. Second, "complications [were] expected," according to the Times. I think so.

One emotion overcame all others when I first read this graphic tale in one of the nation's most read publications: pride. I doubt that any other of my ancestors has ever been featured in The New York Times. I don't think any action would have made me as proud as a successful feud, even if they had. And one that, no less, had the power to change an election! You can take the boy out of Kentucky, but you can't take Kentucky out of the boy, as Mamaw used to say.

What Papaw was thinking is beyond me. Rather than argue with you, Mamaw's family would shoot you. Her father was an intimidating elderly hillbilly with a sailor's mouth and battle decorations. The New York Times featured her grandfather's homicidal deeds because they were so spectacular. Even though her family history was frightening, Mamaw Bonnie was so awful that, decades later, a Marine Corps recruiter would tell me that boot camp would be easier than living at home. He remarked, "Those drill instructors are cruel." "But not like your grandmother." My granddad was not deterred by that cruelty. In 1947, Mamaw and Papaw married in Jackson while teenagers.

There were two kinds of people in Jackson at the time, as the post-World War II euphoria subsided and people started acclimating to a world at peace: those who had uprooted their lives and settled in the industrial powerhouses of the new America, and those who hadn't. My grandparents, who were only fourteen and seventeen years old, had to choose which group to join.

Papaw once told me that for many of his friends, working "in the mines"—mining coal near Jackson—was their only choice. Those who remained in Jackson lived their entire lives on the verge of, if not in, poverty. Papaw relocated to Middletown, a small Ohio town with a fast expanding industrialized economy, shortly after getting married, uprooting his young family.

My grandfather told me this story, which, like most family stories, is mostly factual but omits some important aspects. My great-uncle Arch, Mamaw's brother-in-law and the last of that generation of Jacksonians, introduced me to Bonnie South while I was recently visiting family in Jackson. She had grown just a hundred yards from Mamaw's childhood house. Bonnie South was Mamaw's greatest friend until she moved to Ohio. And according to Bonnie South, there was a little more scandal surrounding Mamaw and Papaw departure than any of us were aware of.

Bonnie South and Papaw fell in love in 1946. Whether they were getting ready for an engagement or just killing time together, I'm not sure what this meant in Jackson at the time. Other than describing Papaw as "very handsome," Bonnie didn't have much to say about him. Bonnie South only remembered that Papaw had cheated on her with her best friend, Mamaw, at some time in 1946. Despite the fact that Papaw was sixteen and Mamaw was thirteen, the affair resulted in a pregnancy. The Blanton Brothers, who had already gained a reputation for protecting Mamaw's honor, my formidable, grizzled great-grandfather, and a network of gun-wielding hillbillies who were immediately aware of Bonnie Blanton's pregnancy were among the additional pressures that made this the ideal time to leave Jackson. Most importantly, before Bonnie and Jim Vance had adapted to feeding themselves, they would soon have another mouth to feed. After a sudden move to Dayton, Ohio, Mamaw and Papaw stayed there for a short time before relocating to Middletown permanently.

We all assumed that the daughter was born after Uncle Jimmy, Mamaw and Papaw's eldest child, because Mamaw occasionally mentioned a daughter who passed away in infancy in subsequent years. In the ten years between Uncle Jimmy's birth and my mother's, Mamaw experienced eight miscarriages. However, my sister recently found a birth certificate for "Infant" Vance, an aunt I never met who passed away at such a young age that her birth certificate also includes her death date. During her first week, the baby that brought my grandparents to Ohio died. The baby's heartbroken mother falsified her age on the birth certificate, saying that she was only fourteen at the time and that she couldn't tell the truth because she had a seventeen-year-old husband, lest they send her back to Jackson or put Papaw in jail.

Mamaw's first adult experience ended tragically. I frequently ponder today: Would she have ever left Jackson if she hadn't had the baby? Would she have fled to a faraway country with Jim Vance? A baby who survived only six days may have altered Mamaw's entire life and our family's course.

My ancestors were in Ohio for whatever reason—economic opportunity or family necessity—and there was no turning back. Papaw thus secured employment with Armco, a large steel corporation that actively sought candidates in the coal belt of eastern Kentucky. Towns like Jackson would be inundated with Armco representatives who would genuinely promise a better life to anyone who would relocate north and work in the mills. A unique rule that pushed applicants with a family member employed by Armco to the front of the employment list promoted mass migration. Armco actively pushed the young men from Appalachian Kentucky to bring their extended families, rather than only hiring them.

Several industrial companies used similar tactics, and they seem to have been successful. There were many Middletowns and Jacksons in that age. Researchers have identified two significant migratory waves from Appalachia to the Midwest's industrial powerhouse economies. The first occurred following World War I, when returning veterans in the industrialized mountains of West Virginia, Tennessee, and Kentucky found it very impossible to find employment. It came to an end as Northern economies were severely affected by the Great Depression. The second wave, which was made up of returning soldiers and the rapidly growing number of young adults in Appalachia in the 1940s and 1950s, included my grandparents. The only items the mountains had that the industrial economies of the North needed were coal and hill people, as the economies of West Virginia and Kentucky fell behind those of their neighbors. Both were exported in large quantities from Appalachia.

Because studies usually estimate "net out-migration" (i.e., the total number of individuals who left minus the number of persons who came in), it is difficult to pinpoint exact statistics. The data is skewed since many families moved back and forth frequently. However, it is undeniable that millions of individuals traversed the "hillbilly highway," a moniker that encapsulated the sentiment of Northerners who saw their towns and cities overrun with people just like my grandparents. The migration's magnitude was astounding. Thirteen of every 100 Kentucky residents left the state in the 1950s. Even more emigration occurred in some places: Harlan County, which gained notoriety from an Academy Award-winning documentary about mining strikes, lost 30% of its population due to migration. One million of Ohio's ten million inhabitants were born in Kentucky, West Virginia, or Tennessee in 1960. This excludes the children and grandchildren of migrants who were native hill people and the sizable population of migrants from other parts of the southern Appalachian Mountains. Since the birthrate of hillbillies was typically significantly higher than that of the original population, there were definitely a lot of these offspring and grandkids.

In short, my grandparents' experience was really typical. Important portions of a whole region moved north and set up shop. More evidence needed? Almost every license plate you see on a northbound roadway in Kentucky or Tennessee the day after Thanksgiving or Christmas is from Ohio, Indiana, or Michigan—cars full of transplanted hillbillies coming home for the holidays.

Mamaw's family enthusiastically joined the migrant flow. Pet, Paul, and Gary, three of her seven siblings, relocated to Indiana and found employment in the construction industry. They both ran profitable businesses and amassed substantial fortunes. David, Betty, Teaberry, and Rose remained. Although everyone but David led rather comfortable lives by their community's standards, they all struggled financially. Compared to the four who stayed, the four who departed died on a far higher social rung. As a young man, Papaw understood the hillbilly's best option was to go out.

In their new city, my grandparents were probably not alone. Even though Mamaw and Papaw were cut off from their family, they were scarcely cut off from the rest of Middletown's population. The majority of the city's residents were from Appalachia and had relocated there in search of employment in the new industrial facilities. The large industrial enterprises' family-based employment methods achieved the intended impact, and the outcomes were expected. Almost without warning, new settlements of Appalachian transplants and their families appeared all over the industrial Midwest. According to one research, "Migration transported families and neighborhoods rather than destroying them." My grandparents found themselves in a predicament that was both familiar and novel in Middletown in the 1950s. They were both familiar since they were still surrounded by hillbillies and new because they were separated from the vast Appalachian support system for the first time.

I want to share with you how my grandparents raised a prosperous family, adapted well to their new surroundings, and retired comfortably in the middle class. That's only part of the truth. In all honesty, my grandparents had a difficult time adjusting to their new life and did so for many years.

To begin with, there was a notable stigma associated with those who left the Kentucky hills in search of a better life. "Too big for your britches" is a term used by hillbillies to characterize people who believe they are superior to the stock they came from. My grandparents heard the word from people back home long after they moved to Ohio. There was a strong feeling that they had deserted their family, and it was assumed that they would visit frequently, regardless of their obligations. The following pattern was typical of Appalachian migrants: Over 90% of them would visit "home" at some point in their life, and over 10% would do so roughly once a month. Even though the drive to Jackson in the 1950s took roughly twenty hours, my grandparents made the trip frequently, sometimes on consecutive weekends. Along with many new obligations, economic mobility also brought with it many pressures.

Both sides contributed to that stigma: They were viewed with suspicion by many of their new neighbors. These hillbillies just didn't fit in with the white Ohioan middle class. They accepted their extended relatives into their houses for too long and had too many children. On multiple instances, Mamaw's siblings spent months living with her and Papaw while they looked for decent jobs outside of the hills. To put it another way, native Middletons vehemently disapproved of many aspects of their culture and traditions. The flood of hill people to Detroit is described in one book, Appalachian Odyssey: "It was not just that the Appalachian migrants, as rural strangers 'out of place' in the city, were upsetting to Midwestern, urban whites." Instead, these migrants upended a wide range of preconceived notions that northern whites had about the appearance, speech, and behavior of white people. The unsettling thing about hillbillies was their race. They supposedly belonged to the same racial order (whites) as those who held social, political, and economic dominance on a local and national level. However, hillbillies and the black people from the South who came to Detroit had a lot in common.

One of Papaw's close friends, a Kentucky hillbilly he met in Ohio, ended up working as a mail carrier in their community. The mail carrier and the Middletown government got into a heated argument shortly after he moved because of the hens he kept in his yard. When his flock of chickens became too big, he would take some of the older ones, wring their necks, and cut them up for meat in his backyard. He treated them the same way Mamaw had treated her hens back in the holler. Every morning he gathered all the eggs. Imagine an educated woman looking out the window in horror as her neighbor, who was born in Kentucky, killed squawking hens a few feet away. Even years later, Mamaw's signature wrath, "Fucking zoning laws," could be evoked by mentioning how the city officials banded together against the old mail carrier, whom my sister and I still refer to as "the chicken man." You can give my ruby-red asshole a kiss.

There were further issues brought on by the relocation to Middletown. In Jackson's mountain dwellings, privacy was more ideal than reality. Your neighbors, family, and friends would suddenly show up at your house. Mothers would give their daughters parenting advice. Sons would receive job instructions from their fathers. Brothers-in-law would receive advice from their brothers on how to handle their wives. People learned about family life on the spot, with much help from their neighbors. A man's house was his castle in Middletown.

But Mamaw and Papaw had left the castle uninhabited. They attempted to adapt an old family structure from the hills to a society of nuclear families and solitude. Despite being newlyweds, they had no one to mentor them in marriage. There were no grandparents, aunts, uncles, or cousins to lighten their load, even if they were parents. Papaw's mother, Goldie, was the sole close relative in the area. She was largely unknown to her own child, so Mamaw couldn't have thought less of her for leaving him.

Mamaw and Papaw began adjusting after a few years. Papaw worked on vehicles in his free time, and his coworkers gradually became friends with Mamaw, who became close to the "neighbor lady" (her term for the neighbors she liked) who lived in a nearby apartment. My uncle Jimmy was born in 1951, and they lavished him with their new material possessions. Mamaw would later tell me that Jimmy was able to sit up at two weeks, walk at four months, speak in full phrases shortly after his first birthday, and read classic literature by the age of three. My uncle later admitted this was a small exaggeration. They went to Indianapolis to see Mamaw's siblings and had a picnic with their new acquaintances. Uncle Jimmy described it to me as "a typical middle-class life." Sort of dull by certain standards, but joyful in a way that you only enjoy when you realize what happens if you're not boring.

This is not to imply that everything went without a hitch. They once went to the mall with the holiday crowd to buy Christmas presents, and they let Jimmy go around to find an item he wanted. He recently told me, "They were advertising it on television." It was a plastic dashboard that resembled a jet fighter plane's dash. You may shoot darts or shine a light. Pretending to be a fighter pilot was the main goal.

Jimmy grabbed up the toy and started playing with it after wandering into a pharmacy that just so happened to sell it. The shopkeeper wasn't pleased. He instructed me to set down the toy and exit. Young Jimmy was reprimanded and left outside in the cold until Mamaw and Papaw passed by and inquired if he wanted to enter the pharmacy.

"I am unable to," Jimmy informed his father.

"Why?"

"I simply cannot."

"For now, tell me why."

He gestured to the shopkeeper. "That man told me to go because he was upset with me." I am not permitted to return inside.

Demanding an explanation for the clerk's harsh behavior, Mamaw and Papaw barged in. Jimmy had been playing with an expensive toy, the salesperson explained. As Papaw picked up the item, he said, "This toy?" Papaw threw it to the floor as the clerk nodded. There was complete chaos. "They went nuts," Uncle Jimmy explained. Mom began stealing random items from the shelf and flinging them around, while Dad flung another toy across the store and walked menacingly toward the cashier. "Kick his fucking ass!" she is yelling. Give him a kick in the ass! "I will break your fucking neck if you say another word to my son," Dad says firmly as he leans in to speak to the cashier. I simply wanted to get the hell out of there because this poor guy was so scared. The Vances carried on with their Christmas shopping as if nothing had happened after the man apologized.

So, yeah, Mamaw and Papaw had trouble adjusting, even during their happiest moments. It was another world in Middletown. Papaw was expected to report impolite pharmacy staff to management when he arrived at work. Mamaw was supposed to take care of the kids, make dinner, and do the washing. But a lady who had nearly killed a man at the age of twelve was not a fit for sewing circles, picnics, or door-to-door vacuum salesman. When the children were small and needed regular care, Mamaw had little assistance and nothing else to do with her time. She would recall, decades later, how alone she felt amid the sluggish middletown suburban grind of the mid-1900s. With typical bluntness, she described that historical period as one in which "women were just shit on all the time."

Mamaw had aspirations, but she was never given the opportunity to follow them. Both specifically (her children and grandchildren were the only things she seemed to enjoy in old age) and generally (she watched shows about abused, neglected, and missing children and used what little spare money she had to buy shoes and school supplies for the poorest children in the neighborhood), children were her greatest love. She frequently expressed her hatred of those who abused children, as if she understood the suffering of neglected children on a very intimate level. I've never understood the source of this sentiment—whether it was because she was abused as a child or because she simply felt sad that her childhood had ended so suddenly. There's a story there, but I probably won't hear it. As a voice for those without one, Mamaw hoped to pursue that love as a career as a children's lawyer. Perhaps because she was unaware of the requirements to become an attorney, she never followed through on that desire. Mamaw never went to high school for a day. Before she was able to legally drive a car, she had given birth to and buried a child. Her new way of life provided no support or chance for a prospective law student with three kids and a spouse, even if she had been aware of the necessary requirements. Both of my grandparents had an almost fanatical belief in the American Dream and hard work, despite the failures. Neither believed that status or riches were unimportant in America. For instance, Mamaw held the view that "they're all a bunch of crooks" when it came to politics, but Papaw later became a devoted Democrat. He had no issue with Armco, but because of a long history of labor conflict, he and others shared his hatred of Kentucky's coal firms. According to Papaw and Mamaw, all bad people were affluent, but not all rich people were wicked. Because the Democratic Party stood for the working class, Papaw was a Democrat. Mamaw adopted this mindset: All politicians may be dishonest, but if there were any outliers, they were definitely part of Franklin Delano Roosevelt's New Deal coalition.

They thought reading', writing', Route 23 would take them to the good life that they had never seen;
They didn't know that old highway would lead them to a world of misery

Mamaw and Papaw may have made it out of Kentucky, but they and their children learned the hard way that Route 23 didn't lead where they hoped.

Chapter 3

Jimmy, my mother Bev, and Lori were the three children of Mamaw and Papaw. In 1951, when Mamaw and Papaw were adjusting to their new lives, Jimmy was born. Through a tragic time of horrible luck and many miscarriages, they tried and tried to have more children. Mamaw lived her entire life with the mental scars of nine children lost. I discovered in college that miscarriages can be caused by excessive stress, and that this is particularly true in the early stages of pregnancy. I wonder how many more aunts and uncles I would have now if it weren't for my grandparents' challenging early transition, which was undoubtedly made worse by Papaw's years of heavy drinking. Nevertheless, they persevered through ten unsuccessful pregnancies, and in the end, it paid off: On January 20, 1961, the day of John F. Kennedy's inauguration, Mom was born, and less than two years later, my aunt Lori was born. Mamaw and Papaw stopped there for some reason.

Before his sisters were born, Uncle Jimmy told me, "We were just a happy, normal middle-class family." I recall thinking that it looked like us when I saw Leave It to Beaver on TV. When he initially said this to me, I gave him a careful nod and ignored it. In retrospect, I see that such a statement must seem crazy to the majority of outsiders. Ordinary middle-class parents don't destroy pharmacies because their child is treated rudely by a store employee. However, that is most likely the incorrect criterion to apply. Mamaw and Papaw considered it natural to destroy store stuff and threaten a sales clerk: Scots-Irish Appalachians do that when someone messes with your child. When I questioned Uncle Jimmy later, he said, "What I mean is that they were united, they were getting along with each other." "But yeah, they could go from being completely normal to murderous in a heartbeat, just like everyone else in our family."

After the birth of their daughter Lori, whom I refer to as Aunt Wee, in 1962, any unity they had had early in their marriage started to wane.

Papaw had developed a drinking habit by the middle of the 1960s, and Mamaw started to isolate herself from the outer world. The mailman was cautioned by local children to stay away from McKinley Street's "evil witch." A huge woman with an extra-long menthol cigarette hanging out of her lips urged the mailman to stay the fuck off her property after he disregarded their instructions. The term "hoarder" had not yet become commonplace, but Mamaw was one, and as she distanced herself from the outside world, her inclinations only grew worse. The house was overflowing with trash; one bedroom was filled with baubles and trash of no earthly worth.

It seems Mamaw and Papaw had two lives throughout this time. There was public life outside. It involved getting the kids ready for school and working during the day. Everyone else witnessed this life, and it was a very successful one by all accounts: My grandmother lived in a house that was a mansion by Jackson standards—two thousand square feet, four bedrooms, and modern plumbing—my grandfather made a salary that was nearly unthinkable to friends back home, he enjoyed his job and did it well, and their kids attended well-funded, contemporary schools.

Life at home was different. Uncle Jimmy recounted, "As a teenager, I didn't notice it at first." You're so preoccupied with your personal affairs at that age that you barely notice the shift. However, it was present. Mom stopped cleaning the house; there were dirty dishes and trash all over the place; Dad went out more. They engaged in much more combat. It was a difficult period overall.

Hillbilly culture at the time (and perhaps today) combined strange sexism, a strong sense of honor, and a strong commitment to family into a potentially explosive concoction. Mamaw's brothers had been prepared to kill boys who disregarded their sister before she got married. They accepted actions that would have resulted in Papaw's death in the holler, now that she was married to a guy that many of them viewed as more of a brother than an outsider. Uncle Jimmy explained, "Mom's brothers would come up and want to go carousing with Dad." They would chase women while intoxicated. Uncle Pet was

25

always in charge. Although I always did, I didn't want to hear about it. The prevailing culture at the time assumed that men would go out and pursue their own interests.

Mamaw was very hurt by the betrayal. Anything that suggested she abhorred a lack of total dedication to family. In her own home, she would say things like "You know I love you, but I'm just a crazy bitch" and "I'm sorry, I'm so damned mean." However, she would lose it if she heard someone from outside the company criticizing even her socks. "Those people are strangers to me. You never discuss family with a stranger. Never. Lindsay, my sister, and I could argue endlessly in her house, and she would generally let us work things out on our own. However, if I told a friend that Mamaw overheard my sister being hateful, she would recall and inform me that I had committed the cardinal sin of disloyalty the next time we were alone. "You have no right to talk about your sister to such a small group of people. You won't even recognize his goddamned name in five years. However, the only real buddy you will ever have is your sister. However, in her own life, her husband and brothers, who ought to have been her most devoted supporters, plotted against her while she had three children at home.

With occasionally amusing outcomes, Papaw appeared to defy the social norms of a middle-class father. After telling his kids he was going to the store and asking if they needed anything, he would return with a brand-new vehicle. One month, a brand-new Chevrolet convertible. Next, an opulent Oldsmobile. They would question him, "Where did you get that?" He would casually respond, "I traded for it, so it's mine."

However, there were moments when his refusal to fit in had disastrous results. Upon their father's return from work, my mother and my little aunt would play a game. On certain days, he would park his car carefully, and the game would proceed smoothly. Their father would enter, they would have supper together as a family, and they would joke around with each other. But on many days, he wouldn't park his car properly; instead, he would back into a spot too fast, carelessly leave his car on the road, or even side-swipe a telephone pole while he was moving. The game was already lost in those days. Mamaw would be informed by Mom and Aunt Wee that Papaw had returned home intoxicated. They would occasionally sneak out the back door and spend the night with Mamaw's pals. At other occasions, Mom and Aunt Wee would prepare for a long night since Mamaw would insist on staying. Papaw ordered a new dinner when he returned home intoxicated one Christmas Eve. That didn't happen, so he grabbed the family's Christmas tree and tossed it out the back door. He coughed up a massive wad of phlegm at everyone's feet as he greeted the throng at his daughter's birthday party the next year. Then he grinned and went to get another beer for himself.

I was shocked to learn that Papaw, who I had loved as a youngster, was such a violent alcoholic. Mamaw's temperament was at least partially to blame for his actions. She wasn't intoxicated, but she was violent. And she used her frustrations to fuel the most fruitful endeavor she could think of: secret warfare. She used scissors to cut Papaw's slacks when he passed out on the couch, causing them to pop at the seam the next time he sat down. Or, to annoy him, she would take his wallet and conceal it in the oven. She would meticulously arrange a tray of fresh garbage whenever he ordered a fresh dinner after work. She would fight back if he was feeling aggressive. To put it briefly, she dedicated her life to making his inebriated existence as miserable as possible.

If Jimmy's youth temporarily protected him from the indications that their marriage was failing, the issue quickly reached a clear low point. "I could hear the furniture bumping and bumping, and they were really getting into it," Uncle Jimmy said when recalling one altercation. Both of them were yelling. I begged them to stop when I walked downstairs. However, they continued. Mamaw picked up a vase of flowers, threw it, and, with her legendary arm, struck Papaw square in the eyes. When he got into his car and drove away, his forehead was slashed open and he was bleeding profusely. I was thinking about that when I got to school the following day.

After a particularly rough night of drinking, Mamaw threatened to murder Papaw if he ever returned home intoxicated. He returned home intoxicated a week later and dozed off on the couch. Never one to lie, Mamaw calmly went to the garage, got a can of gasoline, poured it all over her husband, lit a match, and then dropped it on his chest. Their eleven-year-old daughter acted quickly to extinguish the fire and save Papaw's life when it erupted. Papaw miraculously escaped the incident with only minor burns.

They had to keep their two lives apart since they were hill people. The family conflict couldn't be known to outsiders, and outsiders are defined extremely loosely. Jimmy got a job at Armco when he turned eighteen and moved out right away. Shortly after his departure, Papaw punched Aunt Wee in the face while she was involved in one very heated argument. Despite being an accident, the hit left a terrible black eye. Aunt Wee had to hide in the basement when Jimmy, her own brother, came home for a visit. Jimmy was not supposed to be aware of the inner workings of the house because he no longer lived with the family. Aunt Wee remarked, "That's just the way everyone, especially Mamaw, handled things." "It was simply too humiliating."

Nobody can clearly see why Mamaw and Papaw's marriage failed. Maybe his drunkenness overcame Papaw. Uncle Jimmy believes he "ran around" on Mamaw in the end. Or perhaps Mamaw simply lost it—who could have blamed her for having three alive children, one deceased, and numerous miscarriages in between?

Mamaw and Papaw remained calmly optimistic about their children's futures despite their tumultuous marriage. They reasoned that their children (and grandkids) should have no trouble going to college and obtaining a piece of the American Dream if they could move from a one-room schoolhouse in Jackson to a two-story suburban home with the conveniences of the middle class. They certainly had more money than the relatives who had remained in Kentucky. As children, they never traveled beyond Cincinnati, but as adults, they went to the Atlantic Ocean and Niagara Falls. They thought they had succeeded and that their kids would succeed even more.

But such approach had a really naive quality. Their turbulent family lives had a significant impact on all three kids. Rather than working in the steel mill, Papaw encouraged Jimmy to pursue an education. If Jimmy were to get a full-time job after high school, he cautioned, the money would be like a drug—it would feel wonderful right away, but it would prevent him from accomplishing the things he should be doing. Papaw even stopped Jimmy from putting him on his Armco application as a referral. The chance to leave a house where your mother threw vases at your father's forehead was something that Armco provided that Papaw didn't value.

The main reason Lori suffered in school was because she never showed up for class. Mamaw used to make a joke about how Lori would somehow beat her home when she dropped her off at school. Lori's boyfriend stole some PCP during her sophomore year of high school, and the two of them went back to Mamaw's to indulge. He informed me that because he was larger, he ought to do more. I didn't recall anything else after that. When Mamaw and her friend Kathy put Lori in a cold bathtub, Lori woke up. Meanwhile, her partner was not answering. The young man was not breathing, as far as Kathy could tell. She was told by Mamaw to drag him across the street to the park. She declared, "I don't want him to die in my fucking house." Rather, she summoned someone to transport him to the hospital, where he was kept in critical care for five days.

Lori left high school the following year at age sixteen and married. She was instantly imprisoned in a violent household similar to the one from which she had attempted to flee. To prevent her from visiting her relatives, her new husband would lock her in a bedroom. Aunt Wee later told me, "It was almost like a prison."

Luckily, Jimmy and Lori managed to find their way. Jimmy got a sales position with Johnson & Johnson after working his way through night school. In my family, he was the first to have a "career." Lori was working in radiology by the time she turned thirty, and her new spouse was so charming that Mamaw said to the whole family, "I'm following him if they ever get divorced."

Regretfully, the Vance family was caught up in the statistics, and my mother, Bev, didn't fare well. She left home early, just like her siblings. She was a bright student, but she decided to put off going to college after becoming pregnant at the age of 18. She married her partner after high school and made an effort to start a family. She had learned the lessons of her childhood all too well, though, so she wasn't exactly interested in getting married. Mom filed for divorce and became a single mother after her new life started to exhibit the same drama and arguments as her previous one. At nineteen, she had no spouse, no degree, and a tiny child named Lindsay, who was my sister.

Eventually, Mamaw and Papaw managed to get their act together. In 1983, Papaw made the decision to give up alcohol without much fanfare or medical assistance. He just stopped and didn't say much about it. Despite continuing to reside in different homes, he and Mamaw spent almost all of their waking hours together after their separation and eventual reconciliation. They also made an effort to mend the harm they had caused by assisting Lori in leaving her violent marriage. They assisted Bev with childcare and gave her a loan. They paid for her nursing school, provided housing for her, and assisted her during her rehabilitation. The most significant thing they did was to fill the void left by my mom's inability or unwillingness to be the kind of parent they wish they had been to her. Bev may have been let down by Mamaw and Papaw when she was younger. However, they made up for it for the remainder of their lives.

Chapter 4

I was born in late summer 1984, months before Papaw voted for Ronald Reagan, a Republican, for the first and only time. Reagan achieved the largest electoral landslide in contemporary American history after winning sizable chunks of Rust Belt Democrats like Papaw. In the future, Papaw informed me, "I never liked Reagan much." "However, I detested Mondale, that bitch's son." Compared to my backwoods papaw, Reagan's Democratic opponent was a well-educated liberal from the North. Mondale never had a chance, and Papaw never again voted against his favorite "party of the working man" after he left politics.

My heart will always belong to Jackson, Kentucky, but I spent most of my time in Middletown, Ohio. I was born in a town that was very similar to the one my grandparents had moved to forty years before. Since the 1950s, when the influx of migrants on the hillbilly route dropped to a trickle, its population had not changed much. My secondary school opened for classes soon after World War I, long before my grandparents were born, and my primary school was constructed in the 1930s, before they departed Jackson. Although there were concerning indications, Middletown had managed to avoid serious economic issues, and Armco continued to be the town's largest employment. A longtime public school veteran remarked, "We saw ourselves as a really fine community, on par with Shaker Heights or Upper Arlington," likening the Middletown of the past to some of the most prosperous suburbs in Ohio. "Obviously, none of us anticipated what would occur."

Because of its closeness to the Miami River, which drains straight into the Ohio, Middletown is one of Ohio's oldest incorporated towns, having been established in the 1800s. We used to joke as children that our hometown was so generic that no one bothered to give it a proper name: It's a town, it's in the center between Dayton and Cincinnati, so here we are. (It's not alone: Centerville is a few miles away from

Middletown.) Other than that, Middletown is generic. It served as a prime example of the Rust Belt town's economic growth. It is predominantly working-class in terms of socioeconomic status. In terms of race, there are many white people and black people (the latter are the result of a similar large migration), but not many others. Additionally, it has a very conservative culture, however in Middletown, political conservatism and cultural conservatism are not often the same.

The Jackson residents are not so different from the people I grew up with. This is particularly evident at Armco, where the majority of the town's workforce worked. In fact, the workplace used to be a reflection of the Kentucky villages from which many of the workers were originally from. "A sign over a doorway between departments read, 'Leave Morgan County and Enter Wolfe County,'" according to one author. Kentucky followed the Appalachian migration to the city, even down to its county rivalries.

When I was younger, I divided Middletown into three basic geographies. First, the neighborhood around Uncle Jimmy's senior year of high school, which began in 1969. (Mamaw even referred to it as the "new high school" in 2003.) This was where the "rich" kids lived. Well-maintained parks and office buildings coexisted peacefully with spacious residences. If your father practiced medicine, he most likely had a house or office here, if not both. In my ideal world, I would own a property in Manchester Manor, a brand-new neighborhood a mile from the high school where a good house would cost less than 5% of what a good one in San Francisco would. Subsequently, the impoverished children—the extremely impoverished children—lived close to Armco, where even the lovely houses had been transformed into multifamily apartments. Until recently, I was unaware that this neighborhood was truly divided into two areas: the poorest white residents of Middletown lived in one neighborhood, while the black working-class residents lived in the other. There stood a few housing projects in Middletown.

Then there was the neighborhood where we resided, which was primarily made up of single-family homes with factories and abandoned warehouses close by. In retrospect, I'm not sure if my block and the "really poor" neighborhoods were any different, or if these distinctions were the result of a mindset that didn't want to accept that it was truly impoverished.

Miami Park, a single city block with a swing set, a tennis court, a baseball field, and a basketball court, located across the street from our house. As I became older, I saw that the city had ceased patching up the gaps and changing the nets on the basketball courts, and the lines on the tennis courts were getting thinner every month. The tennis court was reduced to a cement block with patches of grass when I was still a child. I discovered that after two bikes were taken during the week, our neighborhood had "gone downhill." Mamaw claimed that her kids had been safely leaving their bikes unchained in the yard for years. When her grandchildren woke up, they discovered that dead-bolt cutters had split her thick hair in two. I started walking from there. The writing was on the wall almost quickly after my birth, if Middletown had altered much by then. Because the impact has been gradual—more erosion than mudslides—even locals may have missed it. "Geez, Middletown is not looking good" is a typical theme among those of us who visit occasionally, but it's evident if you know where to look.

A thriving shopping mall, eateries that had been around since before World War II, and a few bars where guys like Papaw would congregate and have a beer (or several) after a demanding day at the steel mill were all features of Middletown's proud, almost picturesque downtown in the 1980s. My favorite store was the neighborhood Kmart, which was the focal point of a strip mall close to a Dillman's, a three- or four-location local grocer. The strip mall is now largely empty: Kmart is deserted, and the Dillman family shut down that large business along with the others. When I last looked, the only businesses in what used to be a bustling Middletown center were an Arby's, a cheap grocery shop, and a Chinese buffet. That strip mall site is hardly unusual. Businesses in Middletown are struggling, and many have shut down completely. There were two malls in the area twenty years ago. Even though it still has a few retailers, one of those malls is now a parking lot, and the other is a senior walking course.

Middletown's downtown is essentially a holdover from the heyday of American industry. The intersection of Main Street and Central Avenue in the center of downtown is lined by shuttered stores. As far as I'm aware, Richie's pawn shop has long ago closed, but a repulsive yellow and green sign still stands there. Not far from Richie's is an old drugstore that used to serve root beer floats and have a soda bar. One of those enormous triangle signs that reads "ST___L" because the letters in the middle were broken and never rebuilt is located across the street from a structure that appears to be a theater. Downtown Middletown is the best area to find a cash-for-gold store or a payday lender.

The Sorg Mansion is not far from the main thoroughfare with boarded-up windows and vacant businesses. In the nineteenth century, the Sorgs were a wealthy and influential industrial family that ran a sizable paper mill in Middletown. They helped transform Middletown into a reputable enough city to draw Armco, and they gave enough money to have their names attached to the neighborhood opera theater. Near a once-proud Middletown country club is their mansion, a massive manor house. Despite its splendor, a Maryland couple for $225,000, which is roughly half of what a good multi-room apartment in Washington, D.C., costs recently bought the mansion.

The Sorg Mansion, which is literally on Main Street, is close to several lavish residences that once belonged to Middletown's affluent residents. The majority are now in disrepair. The poorest people of Middletown now live in tiny apartments in those that haven't been partitioned. Once Middletown's pride, the street now serves as a gathering place for drug dealers and users. Nowadays, you stay away from Main Street after dark.

This shift is a sign of growing residential segregation, a new economic reality. White working-class residents in high-poverty areas are becoming more numerous. A quarter of white children lived in an area with a poverty rate above 10 percent in 1970. That percentage was 40% in 2000. Today, it's probably even higher. "Compared to 2000, residents of extreme-poverty neighborhoods in 2005–09 were more likely to be white, native-born, high school or college graduates, homeowners, and not receiving public assistance," according to a 2011 Brookings Institution study. To put it another way, poor areas are no longer limited to urban ghettos; they have extended to the suburbs.

Complicated factors have led to this. From George W. Bush's ownership society to Jimmy Carter's Community Reinvestment Act, federal housing policy has aggressively promoted homeownership. However, there is a high social cost associated with homeownership in the Middletowns of the world: People are trapped in particular neighborhoods by dropping home values as jobs depart in a particular location. Since the market has collapsed and you now owe more than any buyer is prepared to pay, you are unable to move, even if you would like to. Many people choose to remain where they are because relocation is so expensive. Naturally, individuals with the least amount of money are typically the ones that are stranded; those who can afford to escape do so.

City officials have made fruitless attempts to revitalize Middletown's downtown. Following Central Avenue to its terminus on the banks of the Miami River, which was once a beautiful location, will lead you to their most notorious endeavor. The city's brain trust chose to transform our lovely riverside into Lake Middletown for reasons I cannot fathom. This infrastructure project reportedly involved dumping tons of gravel into the river in the hopes that something intriguing would emerge. Although the river now has a man-made mud island roughly the size of a city block, it achieved nothing.

I always thought it was pointless to try to revitalize downtown Middletown. Because our downtown lacked hip cultural amenities, people stayed. Middletown didn't have enough customers to sustain the trendy cultural offerings, so they left. And why weren't more profitable customers? because those consumers could not be employed in enough jobs. The problems in downtown Middletown were a sign of everything else that was going on with the residents of Middletown, particularly the decline in significance of Armco Kawasaki Steel.

Armco Steel and Kawasaki, the same Japanese company that produces those little, powerful motorcycles (or "crotch rockets," as us kids used to call them), merged to form AK Steel in 1989. For two reasons, most people still call it Armco. The first is that "Armco built this fucking town," as Mamaw said. She was telling the truth when she said Armco funds were used to purchase several of the city's greatest parks and amenities. In addition to helping fund the schools, Armco employees served on the boards of other significant local organizations. Thousands of Middletons were employed by it, and despite their lack of formal education, they made decent wages, just like my grandfather did.

Armco's reputation was built on meticulous design. "Until the 1950s, the 'big four' employers of the Miami Valley region—Procter and Gamble in Cincinnati, Champion Paper and Fiber in Hamilton, Armco Steel in Middletown, and National Cash Register in Dayton—had had peaceful labor relations, in part because they... [hired] family and friends of employees who were once migrants themselves," writes Chad Berry in his book Southern Migrants, Northern Exiles. For instance, 117 of the 220 Kentuckyians employed by Middletown's Inland Container were from Wolfe County alone. Much of the goodwill that Armco (and comparable corporations) had created persisted, even though labor relations had undoubtedly deteriorated by the 1980s.

Kawasaki was a Japanese firm, and in a town full of World War II veterans and their families, you would think that General Tojo himself had chosen to establish himself in southwest Ohio when the merger was announced. This is another reason most people still call it Armco. The opposition mainly consisted of noise. A few days after they announced the merger, even Papaw, who previously threatened to disown his children if they purchased a Japanese car, ceased griping. In actuality, he informed me, "the Japanese are now our friends." It will be the goddamned Chinese if we have to fight any of those nations.

The Kawasaki deal symbolized an unpleasant reality: American manufacturing was a challenging industry in the post-globalization era. Businesses like Armco would need to retool if they wanted to survive. Armco was given a chance by Kawasaki, and without it, Middletown's leading business most likely would not have survived.

My buddies and I were unaware that the world had changed when we were growing up. Papaw had a large pension, stock in Armco, and had retired just a few years before. Access to Armco Park, the town's most upscale and exclusive leisure area, was considered a status symbol, indicating that your father (or grandfather) was a well-respected professional. I never realized that Armco, which provides free concerts, parks, and scholarship financing, wouldn't be around for very long.

Few of my friends, however, aspired to work there. We shared the same childhood aspirations as other kids. We wanted to be action heroes, football stars, or astronauts. At the time, I thought it was quite fair to pursue a career as a professional puppy-player-wither. By sixth grade, we aspired to work as doctors, veterinarians, preachers, or entrepreneurs. Not steelworkers, though. Nobody sought a blue-collar job and its promise of a decent middle-class life, even at Roosevelt Elementary, where most people's parents were not college educated due to Middletown geography. We took Armco for granted and never thought we'd be lucky to get a job there.

Many kids today seem to feel that way. I had a conversation with Jennifer McGuffey, a teacher at Middletown High School who works with at-risk students, a few years ago. She shook her head and said, "A lot of students just don't understand what's out there." Because the coach treats them badly, some children who want to play baseball never even make it onto the high school squad. Then there are individuals who are struggling academically, and when you try to discuss their future plans with them, they bring up AK. "Oh, I can work at AK." There, my uncle works. It seems as though they are unable to relate the state of affairs in this town to the dearth of employment at AK. My first thought was: How could these children not comprehend the nature of the world? They saw their town change right in front of their eyes, didn't they? But then I understood: Why would they, because we didn't?

My grandparents came from the Kentucky hills to the middle class in America thanks to Armco, which was their economic savior. My granddad knew every make and model of automobile made of Armco steel and adored the company. Papaw would visit used car dealerships whenever he saw an old Ford or Chevy, even after the majority of American automakers had moved away from steel-bodied vehicles. He would inform me, "Armco made This steel." It was one of the rare occasions when he showed true pride.

"Your generation will make its living with their minds, not their hands," he once told me, demonstrating his lack of interest in my employment there despite his pride. At Armco, being an engineer was the only legitimate career path—not working as a welder. It must have been the same for many other parents and grandparents in Middletown: They believed progress was needed for the American Dream. Although manual labor was a noble profession, we needed to do something new because it was the work of their generation. Moving up meant moving on. That meant attending college.

However, there was no notion that not obtaining a higher degree would cause embarrassment or other repercussions. Teachers didn't tell us that we weren't smart enough or wealthy enough to make it, so the message wasn't clear. However, it pervaded everything, including the air we breathed: We didn't know anyone at a prestigious out-of-state school, our older friends and siblings were perfectly happy to remain in Middletown regardless of their career prospects, no one in our families had attended college, and everyone knew at least one young adult who was either unemployed or underemployed.

Twenty percent of incoming freshmen at Middletown's public high school will not graduate. The majority won't complete college. Almost nobody will attend an out-of-state college. Because those around them don't do much, students don't have high expectations for themselves. Many parents accept this phenomenon. Before Mamaw started to care about my high school academics, I don't recall ever receiving a reprimand for receiving a poor grade. I would hear comments like "Well, maybe she's just not that great at fractions" or "J.D.'s more of a numbers kid, so I wouldn't worry about that spelling test" when my sister and I were having trouble in school.

It was and still is believed that there are two types of people who make it. The first are fortunate since their lives were predetermined from birth and they come from well-to-do households with connections. The second group is meritocratic; they were born smart and couldn't possibly fail. People in Middletown assume that everyone who makes it is simply highly intelligent because so few fit into the former category. For the typical Middletonian, natural skill is more important than hard labor.

It's not like educators and parents don't talk about hard work. They also don't go around shouting that they anticipate their kids to do poorly. These sentiments are hidden beneath the surface, manifested more in actions than in words. A lifetime welfare recipient, one of our neighbors would ramble on about the value of hard work in between begging my grandma to let her drive or offering to exchange food stamps for cash at a premium. She would remark that because so many people misuse the system, industrious people cannot get the assistance they require. This was the mental model she had created: Although she had never worked in her life, she was a clear exception to the rule that the system's beneficiaries were lavish moochers.

In areas like Middletown, people talk about hard labor all the time. Nobody in a place where thirty percent of the young men work less than twenty hours a week is conscious of their own indolence. A report on working-class whites was released during the 2012 election season by the left-leaning think organization Public Religion Institute. Among other things, it discovered that whites from the working class put in more hours at work than whites with college degrees. However, it is clearly untrue that the typical white working-class person puts in more hours. The Public Religion Institute used surveys as the basis for its findings. In other words, they called people and asked them what they believed. The report just demonstrates that many people talk about working more than they actually do.

Naturally, there are many complex reasons why the poor don't work as much as others, and it's too simple to attribute the issue to laziness. Because the Arms of the world are going out of business and their skill sets don't mesh well in the modern economy, many people have no other option except to work part-time. However, for whatever reason, the rhetoric of hard effort is at odds with the actual situation. Middletown's children struggle with and are absorbed by that battle.

The Scots-Irish migrants are similar to their relatives back in the lowlands in this and many other ways. The patriarch of a sizable Appalachian family introduces himself in an HBO documentary on the hill people of eastern Kentucky by making clear distinctions between work that is appropriate for males and work that is appropriate for women. It's evident what he views as "women's work," but it's unclear what work, if any, he finds acceptable. Given that the man has never held a paying job in his life, it appears to be unpaid work. In the end, his own son's assessment is damning: "Daddy claims to have worked throughout his life." His goddamned ass is the only thing that Daddy has worked. Pa, why not tell it as it is? Daddy drank too much. He didn't bring food home, and he would remain intoxicated. Mommy provided for her children. Had it not been for Mommy, we would have perished.

These contradictory standards regarding the importance of blue-collar employment coexisted with a widespread lack of knowledge about how to obtain white-collar work. We were unaware that other children had already begun a competition to succeed in life all around the nation, including in our city. Every morning in first grade, we had a game where the instructor would say the number of the day, and we would each reveal a math equation that resulted in the number. Therefore, you may declare "two plus two" and claim a prize—typically a small piece of candy—if the day's number was four. Thirty was the number one day. "Twenty-nine plus one," "twenty-eight plus two," and "fifteen plus fifteen" were the simple answers that the pupils in front of me went over. I was superior to that. The teacher was going to be completely blown away.

When it was my time, I exclaimed, "Fifty minus twenty," with pride. I got two pieces of candy for trying subtraction, a skill we had only acquired a few days earlier, and the teacher was ecstatic. Moments later, as I was beaming with my own genius, a different student exclaimed, "Ten times three." I didn't even know what that meant. Times? Who was this man?

My competitor joyfully gathered not two, but three pieces of candy, and the teacher was even more astonished. The instructor briefly discussed multiplication and asked if anyone else was aware that it even existed. We didn't raise a hand. I, for one, was devastated. When I got home, I started crying. I was positive that some character flaw was the cause of my ignorance. I simply felt foolish.

The fact that I had never heard the word "multiplication" until that day was not my fault. My family didn't spend time working on arithmetic issues, and I hadn't learnt it in school. However, it was a devastating setback for a small child who aspired to succeed in school. I was unable to distinguish between knowledge and intellect due to my undeveloped brain. So I thought I was a fool.

Even though I didn't understand multiplication that day, Papaw transformed my sadness into victory when I told him about it when I got home. Before supper, I studied division and multiplication. After that, my grandfather and I would practice progressively harder arithmetic once a week for two years, rewarding good performance with ice cream. When I didn't grasp an idea, I would scold myself and walk away feeling disappointed. However, Papaw would always be ready to go again after I pouted for a few minutes. Despite my lack of aptitude for math, Mom took me to the public library before I could read, obtained a library card, taught me how to use it, and always made sure I had access to children's books at home.

To put it another way, I got a different message at home in spite of all the environmental influences from my town and neighborhood. And I might have been spared by that.

Chapter 5

One of the questions I loathed, and that adults always asked, was whether I had any brothers or sisters. When you're a kid, you can't just wave your hand, say, "It's complicated," and move on. And unless you're a particularly skilled sociopath, dishonesty can only get you so far. So for a while, I dutifully answered, guiding people through the tangled web of family relationships to which I'd grown accustomed. I had a biological half-brother and half-sister whom I never saw because my biological father gave me up for adoption. I had many stepbrothers and stepsisters by one measure, but only two if you limited the count to the offspring of my mother's current husband. Then there was my biological father's wife, and she had at least one child, so maybe I should count him too. Sometimes I'd get philosophical about the meaning of the word "sibling": Are the children of your mother's former husbands still related to you? If so, what about the future children of your mother's former husbands? By some measures, I probably had about a dozen stepsiblings.

There was one person for whom the term "sibling" definitely applied: my sister, Lindsay. If an adjective ever preceded her introduction, it was always one of pride: "my full sister, Lindsay"; "my whole sister, Lindsay"; "my big sister, Lindsay". Lindsay was (and remains) the person I was most proud to know. The moment I learned that "half-sister" had nothing to do with my affection and everything to do with the genetic nature of our relationship-that Lindsay, by virtue of having a different father, was as much my half-sister as people I'd never seen-remains one of the most devastating moments of my life. Mamaw told me this nonchalantly as I was getting out of the shower one night before bedtime, and I screamed and wailed as if I'd just learned that my dog had died. I calmed down only after Mamaw relented and agreed that no one would ever refer to Lindsay as my "half-sister" again.

Lindsay Leigh was five years older than me, born just two months after Mamaw graduated high school. I was obsessed with her, both in the way that all children adore their older siblings and in a way that was unique to our circumstances. Her heroism on my behalf was legendary. Once, after she and I fought over a soft pretzel, resulting in Mom dropping me off in an empty parking lot to show Lindsay what life would be like without me, it was my sister's fit of grief and rage that immediately brought Mom back. During explosive fights between Mom and any man she let into our home, it was Lindsay who retreated to her bedroom to make a distress call to Mamaw and Papaw. She fed me when I was hungry, changed my diaper when no one else would, and dragged me everywhere with her-even though, as Mamaw and Aunt Wee told me, I weighed almost as much as she did.

I always thought of her more as an adult than a child. She never expressed her displeasure with her teenage boyfriends by storming off and slamming doors. When Mom was working late or otherwise couldn't make it home, Lindsay would make sure we had something for dinner. I teased her the way all little brothers tease their sisters, but she never yelled at me, screamed at me, or made me afraid of her. In one of my most shameful moments, for reasons I can't remember, I wrestled Lindsay to the ground. I was ten or eleven, which would have made her about fifteen, and although I realized then that I'd outgrown her in strength, I continued to think there was nothing childish about her. She was above all, the "only real adult in the house," as Papaw would say, and my first line of defense, even before Mamaw. She made dinner when she had to, did the laundry when no one else would, and rescued me from the back of that police car. I was so dependent on her that I didn't see Lindsay for what she was: a young girl, not old enough to drive, learning to take care of herself and her little brother at the same time.

That began to change the day our family decided to give Lindsay a chance to follow her dreams. Lindsay was always a beautiful girl. When my friends and I ranked the prettiest girls in the world, I listed Lindsay first, just ahead of Demi Moore and Pam Anderson. Lindsay had heard about a modeling recruitment event at a Dayton hotel, so Mom, Mamaw, Lindsay, and I piled into Mamaw's Buick and headed north. Lindsay was bursting with excitement, and so was I. This was going to be her big break, and by extension, our whole family's big break.

When we arrived at the hotel, a lady told us to follow the signs to a huge ballroom and get in line. The ballroom was perfectly tacky in that 1970s way: ugly carpet, big chandeliers, and lights just bright enough to keep you from tripping over your own feet. I wondered how any talent agent could ever appreciate my sister's beauty. It was too damn dark.

Finally, we got to the front of the line. The talent agent seemed optimistic about my sister. She said something about how cute she was and told her to wait in another room. Surprisingly, she said that I was model material, too, and asked if I'd like to follow my sister and hear about our next step. I enthusiastically agreed.

After a short time in the holding room, Lindsay and I and the other selectees learned that we had made it to the next round, but another process awaited us in New York City. The agency staff gave us pamphlets with more information and told us that we needed to RSVP within the next few weeks. On the way home, Lindsay and I were ecstatic. We were going to New York City to become famous models. The fee to go to New York was high, and if someone really wanted us as models, they would probably have paid for our audition. In hindsight, the cursory treatment they gave each individual-each "audition" was no more than a few-sentence conversation-suggests that the whole event was more scam than talent search. But I don't know: Model audition protocol has never been my area of expertise.

What I do know is that our exuberance didn't survive the car ride. Mom started worrying aloud about the cost of the trip, which caused Lindsay and I to argue about which one of us should go (no doubt I was being a brat). Mom got angrier and angrier and then snapped. What happened next was no surprise: There was a lot of yelling, some hitting and driving, and then a stopped car on the side of the road full of two sobbing kids. Mamaw intervened before things got out of hand, but it's a miracle we didn't crash and die: Mom driving, slapping the kids in the back seat; Mamaw on the passenger side, slapping and screaming at Mom. That was why the car stopped - even though Mom was a multitasker, this was too much. We drove home in silence after Mamaw explained that if Mom lost her temper again, Mamaw would shoot her in the face. We stayed at Mamaw's house that night.

I'll never forget Lindsay's face as she marched upstairs to bed. It bore the pain of defeat known only to a person who has experienced the highest highs and the lowest lows in a matter of minutes. She had been on the verge of realizing a childhood dream; now she was just another teenage girl with a broken heart. Mamaw turned to retire to her couch, where she watched Law & Order, read the Bible, and fell asleep. I stood in the narrow hallway that separated the living room from the dining room and asked Mamaw a question that had been on my mind since she ordered Mom to drive us home safely. I knew what she'd say, but I guess I just wanted reassurance. "Mamaw, does God love us?" She hung her head, hugged me, and began to cry.

The question hurt Mamaw because the Christian faith was central to our lives, especially hers. We never went to church, except on rare occasions in Kentucky or when Mamaw decided that what we needed in our lives was religion. Still, Mamaw's was a deeply personal (if quirky) faith. She couldn't say "organized religion" without disdain. She saw churches as breeding grounds for perverts and money changers. And she hated what she called "the loud and proud"-people who wore their faith on their sleeves, always ready to let you know how pious they were. Still, she sent much of her spare income to churches in Jackson, Kentucky, especially those controlled by Reverend Donald Ison, an elderly man who bore a striking resemblance to the priest in The Exorcist.

In Mamaw's estimation, God never left our side. He celebrated with us when times were good and comforted us when they weren't. On one of our many trips to Kentucky, Mamaw tried to merge onto the highway after a quick stop for gas. She didn't pay attention to the signs, so we found ourselves on the wrong side of a one-way exit, with angry drivers swerving to avoid us. I screamed in terror, but after a U-turn on a three-lane interstate, the only thing Mamaw said about the incident was, "We're fine, damn it. Don't you know Jesus rides in the car with me?"

The theology she taught was simple, but it was a message I needed to hear. To coast through life was to waste my God-given talent, so I had to work hard. I had to provide for my family because Christian duty demanded it. I had to forgive, not only for my mother's sake, but mine. I was never to despair because God had a plan.

Mamaw often told a parable: A young man was sitting at home when a terrible rainstorm began. Within hours, the man's house began to flood, and someone came to his door offering a ride to higher ground. The man refused, saying, "God will take care of me. A few hours later, as the water engulfed the first floor of the man's house, a boat passed by and the captain offered to take the man to safety. The man refused, saying, "God will take care of me. A few hours later, as the man waited on his rooftop-his entire home flooded-a helicopter flew by and the pilot offered transportation to dry land. Again, the man refused, telling the pilot that God would look after him. Soon afterward, the waters overtook the man, and as he stood before God in heaven, he protested his fate: "You promised to help me as long as I'm faithful." God replied, "I sent you a car, a boat, and a helicopter. Your death is your own fault. God helps those who help themselves. That was the wisdom of the Book of Mamaw.

The fallen world described by the Christian religion matched the world I saw around me: one where a happy car ride could quickly turn to misery, one where individual misbehavior rippled through the life of a family and a community. When I asked Mamaw if God loved us, I asked her to reassure me that our religion could still make sense of the world we lived in. I needed reassurance of a deeper justice, a cadence or rhythm that lurked beneath the heartache and chaos.

Not long after Lindsay's childhood modeling dream went up in flames, I was in Jackson with Mamaw and my cousin Gail on August 2, my eleventh birthday. Late in the afternoon, Mamaw told me to call Bob - still my legal father - because I hadn't heard from him. He and Mom got divorced after we moved back to Middletown, so it wasn't surprising that he rarely checked in. But my birthday was obviously special, and I thought it was odd that he hadn't called. So I called and got his answering machine. A few hours later, I called again with the same result. I instinctively knew I would never see Bob again.

Either because she felt bad for me or because she knew I loved dogs, Gail took me to the local pet store where a brand-new litter of German Shepherd puppies was on display. I wanted one badly and had just enough birthday money to make the purchase. Gail reminded me that dogs were a lot of work and that my family (read: my mother) had a terrible history of getting dogs and then giving them away. When wisdom fell on deaf ears-"You're probably right, Gail, but they're soooo cute!"-authority kicked in: "Honey, I'm sorry, but I'm not letting you buy that dog." By the time we got back to Mamaw Blanton's house, I was more upset about the dog than I was about losing daddy number two.

I cared less about the fact that Bob was gone than about the disruption his departure would inevitably cause. He was just the latest casualty in a long line of failed father candidates. There was Steve, a soft-spoken man with a temperament to match. I used to pray that Mom would marry Steve because he was nice and had a good job. But they broke up and she moved on to Chip, a local policeman. Chip was a bit of a hillbilly himself: He loved cheap beer, country music, and catfish fishing, and we got along fine until he, too, was gone.

One of the worst parts, frankly, was that Bob's departure would further complicate the tangled web of surnames in our family. Lindsay was a Lewis (her father's last name), Mom took the last name of the husband she was married to, Mamaw and Papaw were Vances, and all of Mamaw's brothers were Blantons. I shared a name with no one I really cared about (which already bothered me), and with Bob gone, explaining why my name was J.D. Hamel would require a few more awkward moments. "Yes, my legal father's last name is Hamel. You don't know him because I don't see him. No, I don't know why I don't see him."

Of all the things I hated about my childhood, nothing compared to the revolving door of father figures. To her credit, Mom had avoided abusive or neglectful partners, and I never felt mistreated by any of the men she brought into our home. But I hated the disruption. And I hated how often these boyfriends would disappear from my life just as I'd begun to like them. Lindsay, with the benefit of age and wisdom, viewed all men skeptically. She knew that eventually they'd be gone. With Bob's departure, I had learned the same lesson.

Mom had brought these men into our lives for the right reasons. She often wondered aloud if Chip or Bob or Steve were good "father figures. She would say: "He takes you fishing, that's really good," or "It's important to learn about manhood from someone closer to your age." When I heard her yelling at one of them, or crying on the floor after a particularly heated argument, or saw her in despair after a breakup, I felt guilty that she was going through this for my sake. After all, I thought, Dad was a good enough father figure. I promised her after every breakup that we'd be okay, or that we'd get through it together, or (echoing Mamaw) that we didn't need any damn men. I know that Mom's motives were not entirely selfless: She (like all of us) was motivated by a desire for love and companionship. But she was also looking out for us.

The road to hell, however, is paved with good intentions. Caught between various father candidates, Lindsay and I never learned how a man should treat a woman. Chip may have taught me how to tie a fishing hook, but I learned little else about what masculinity requires of me other than drinking beer and yelling at a woman when she yells at you. In the end, the only lesson I learned was that you can't depend on people. "I learned that men disappear at the drop of a hat," Lindsay once said. "They don't care about their kids; they don't provide; they just disappear, and it's not that hard to make them go."

Mom may have sensed that Bob was regretting his decision to take on another child, because one day she called me into the living room to talk on the phone with Don Bowman, my biological father. It was a brief but memorable conversation. He asked me if I remembered wanting to have a farm with horses and cows and chickens, and I said I did. He asked if I remembered my siblings - Cory and Chelsea - and I did a little, so I said, "Sort of. He asked if I wanted to see him again. I knew little about my biological father and had little memory of my life before Bob adopted me. I knew that Don had abandoned me because he didn't want to pay child support (or so Mom said). I knew that he was married to a woman named Cheryl, that he was tall, and that people thought I looked like him. And I knew he was, in Mamaw's words, a "Holy Roller. That was the word she used for charismatic Christians who, she claimed, "handled snakes and screamed and wailed in church. That was enough to pique my curiosity: With little religious training, I was eager to experience a real church. I asked Mom if I could see him, and she agreed, so in the same summer that my legal father walked out of my life, my biological father walked back in. Mom had come full circle: After going through a number of men to find me a father, she had settled on the original candidate.

Don Bowman had a lot more in common with Mom's side of the family than I expected. His father (and my grandfather), Don C. Bowman, also migrated from eastern Kentucky to southwestern Ohio for work. After marrying and starting a family, my grandfather Bowman died suddenly, leaving behind two young children and a young wife. My grandmother remarried, and Dad spent much of his childhood in eastern Kentucky with his grandparents.

More than anyone, Dad understood what Kentucky meant to me because it meant the same thing to him. His mother remarried early, and although her second husband was a good man, he was also very strict and an outsider-even the best step parents take some getting used to. In Kentucky, among his people and with plenty of space, Dad could be himself. I felt the same way. There were two kinds of people: those I acted around because I wanted to impress them, and those I acted around to avoid embarrassing myself. The latter people were outcasts, and Kentucky had none of them.

In many ways, Dad's life project was to rebuild for himself what he once had in Kentucky. When I first visited him, Dad had a modest house on a beautiful piece of land, fourteen acres in all. There was a medium-sized pond with fish, a couple of fields for cows and horses, a barn, and a chicken coop. Every morning the children would run to the chicken coop and grab the morning's haul of eggs-usually seven or eight, a perfect number for a family of five. During the day we roamed the property with a dog in tow, catching frogs and chasing rabbits. It was exactly what Dad had done as a child, and exactly what I did with Mamaw in Kentucky.

I remember running through a field with Dad's collie, Dannie, a beautiful, bedraggled creature so gentle that he once caught a baby rabbit and carried it unharmed in his mouth to a human for inspection. I have no idea why I ran, but we both collapsed from exhaustion and lay in the grass, Dannie's head on my chest and my eyes staring up at the blue sky. I don't know if I'd ever felt so content, so completely unconcerned about life and its stresses.

Dad had built a house with an almost disconcerting serenity. He and his wife argued, but they rarely raised their voices to each other and never resorted to the brutal insults that were commonplace in Mom's house. None of their friends drank, even socially. Although they believed in corporal punishment, it was never excessive or combined with verbal abuse - the spanking was methodical and without anger. My younger brother and sister clearly enjoyed their lives, even if they lacked pop music and R-rated movies.

What little I knew of Dad's character during his marriage to Mom came mostly secondhand. Mamaw, Aunt Wee, Lindsay, and Mom all told varying degrees of the same story: that Dad was mean. He yelled a lot and sometimes hot Mom. Lindsay told me that I had a strangely large and misshapen head as a child, and she attributed it to a time when she saw Dad aggressively pushing Mom.

Dad denies ever physically abusing anyone, including Mom. My guess is that they were physically abusive to each other in the way that Mom and most of her husbands were: a little pushing, a little plate throwing, but nothing more. What I do know is that between the end of his marriage to Mom and the beginning of his marriage to Cheryl - which happened when I was four - Dad had changed for the better. He credits a more serious commitment to his faith. In this, Dad embodied a phenomenon that social scientists have observed for decades: Religious people are much happier. Regular churchgoers commit fewer crimes, are in better health, live longer, make more money, drop out of high school less often, and graduate from college more often than those who don't attend church at all. MIT economist Jonathan Gruber even found that the relationship is causal: It's not just that people who happen to lead successful lives go to church; it's that church seems to promote good habits.

In his religious habits, Dad lived up to the stereotype of a culturally conservative Protestant with Southern roots, though the stereotype is mostly inaccurate. Despite their reputation for religious devotion, the people back home were more like Mamaw than Dad: deeply religious, but without any attachment to a real church community. In fact, the only conservative Protestants I knew who attended church regularly were my father and his family. In the middle of the Bible Belt, active church attendance is actually quite low.

Despite its reputation, Appalachia-especially northern Alabama and Georgia to southern Ohio-has far lower church attendance than the Midwest, parts of the Mountain West, and much of the space between Michigan and Montana. Oddly, we think we attend church more than we actually do. In a recent Gallup poll, Southerners and Midwesterners reported the highest rates of church attendance in the country. Yet actual church attendance is much lower in the South.

This pattern of deception has to do with cultural pressures. In southwestern Ohio, where I was born, both the Cincinnati and Dayton metropolitan areas have very low church attendance rates, about the same as ultra-liberal San Francisco. No one I know in San Francisco would be ashamed to admit that they don't go to church. (In fact, some of them might be ashamed to admit that they do.) Ohio is the opposite. Even as a kid, I'd lie when people asked me if I attended church regularly. According to Gallup, I wasn't alone in feeling that pressure. The juxtaposition is jarring: Religious institutions remain a positive force in people's lives, but in a part of the country battered by declining manufacturing, unemployment, addiction, and broken homes, church attendance has declined. Dad's church offered something that people like me desperately needed. For alcoholics, it provided a community of support and a sense that they weren't fighting their addiction alone. For expectant mothers, it offered a free home with job training and parenting classes. If someone needed a job, church friends could either provide one or make an introduction. When Dad was struggling financially, his church rallied to buy a used car for the family. In the broken world I saw around me-and for the people struggling in that world-religion offered tangible help to keep believers on track.

I was drawn to Dad's faith, even though I learned early on that it had played a significant role in the adoption that led to our long separation. While I enjoyed the time we spent together, the pain of that adoption remained, and we often talked about how and why it happened in the first place. For the first time, I heard his side of the story: that the adoption had nothing to do with a desire to avoid child support, and that far from simply "giving me away," as Mom and Mamaw had said, Dad had hired several lawyers and done everything possible to keep me.

He worried the custody battle would destroy me. When I saw him during pre adoption visitations, I would hide under the bed for the first few hours, afraid he would kidnap me and never let me see Mamaw again. Seeing his son in such a frightened state made him rethink his approach. Mamaw hated him, a fact I knew firsthand. But Dad said her hatred stemmed from the early days of his marriage to Mom, when he was far from a perfect husband. Sometimes when he came to pick me up, Mamaw would stand on the porch and stare at him, unblinking, clutching a hidden gun. When he spoke with the court's child psychiatrist, he learned that I had begun acting out at school and was showing signs of emotional problems. (I know this is true. After a few weeks in kindergarten, I was held back for a year. Two decades later, I ran into the teacher who had endured my first foray into kindergarten. She told me that I had behaved so badly that she'd almost quit teaching - three weeks into her first year. That she remembered me twenty years later says a lot about my misbehavior).

Finally, Dad told me, he asked God for three signs that adoption was in my best interest. Those signs apparently came, and I became the legal son of Bob, a man I'd known for barely a year. I don't doubt the truth of this account, and while I sympathize with the obvious difficulty of the decision, I've never been comfortable with the idea of leaving the fate of your child up to signs from God.

Still, this was a small bump in the road, all things considered. Just knowing that he cared for me erased a lot of childhood pain. Overall, I loved my father and his church. I'm not sure if I liked the structure or just wanted to be a part of something that was important to him- both, I suppose-but I became a devoted convert. I devoured books on young-earth creationism and joined online chat rooms to challenge scientists on evolution. I learned about millennial prophecy and convinced myself that the world would end in 2007. I even dumped my Black Sabbath CDs. Dad's church encouraged all of this because it questioned the wisdom of secular science and the morality of secular music.

Despite the lack of a legal relationship, I began to spend a lot of time with Dad. I visited him on most holidays and spent every other weekend at his house. Although I loved seeing aunts, uncles, and cousins who hadn't been a part of my life for years, the basic separation of my two lives remained. Dad avoided Mom's side of the family, and vice versa. Lindsay and Mamaw appreciated Dad's new role in my life, but they continued to distrust him. To Mamaw, Dad was the "sperm donor" who had abandoned me at a critical juncture. Although I, too, resented Dad for the past, Mamaw's stubbornness didn't make things any easier.

Nevertheless, my relationship with Dad continued to evolve, as did my relationship with his church. The downside of his theology was that it encouraged a certain isolation from the outside world. I couldn't listen to Eric Clapton at Dad's house - not because the lyrics were inappropriate, but because Eric Clapton was influenced by demonic forces. I'd heard people joke that if you played Led Zeppelin's "Stairway to Heaven" backwards you'd hear an evil incantation, but a member of Dad's church talked about the Zeppelin myth as if it were actually true.

These were quirks, and at first I understood them as little more than strict rules that I could either obey or circumvent. But I was a curious kid, and the deeper I delved into evangelical theology, the more I felt compelled to distrust many areas of society. Evolution and the Big Bang became ideologies to be confronted, not theories to be understood. Many of the sermons I heard spent as much time criticizing other Christians as anything else. Theological battle lines were drawn, and those on the other side weren't just wrong about interpreting the Bible, they were somehow unchristian. I admired my Uncle Dan above all other men, but when he spoke of his Catholic acceptance of evolution, my admiration became tinged with suspicion. My new faith had put me on the lookout for heretics. Good friends who interpreted parts of the Bible differently were bad influences. Even Mamaw fell out of favor because her religious views didn't conflict with her affinity for Bill Clinton.

As a young teenager, thinking seriously for the first time about what I believed and why I believed it, I had an acute sense that the walls were closing in on "real" Christians. There was talk of the "War on Christmas"-which, as far as I could tell, consisted mostly of ACLU activists suing small towns for Nativity displays. I read a book called Persecution by David Limbaugh about the various ways Christians were discriminated against. The Internet was abuzz with talk of New York art displays that featured images of Christ or the Virgin Mary covered in feces. For the first time in my life, I felt like a persecuted minority.

All this talk about Christians who weren't Christian enough, secularists indoctrinating our youth, art exhibits insulting our faith, and persecution by the elites made the world a scary and strange place. Take gay rights, a particularly hot topic among conservative Protestants. I'll never forget the time I convinced myself I was gay. I was eight or nine, maybe younger, and I stumbled upon a broadcast by a fire-and-brimstone preacher. The man was talking about the evils of homosexuals, how they had infiltrated our society, and how they were all destined for hell unless they seriously repented. At the time, the only thing I knew about homosexuals was that they preferred men to women. That described me perfectly: I hated girls, and my best friend in the world was my buddy Bill. Oh no, I'm going to hell.

I broached the subject with Mamaw and confessed that I was gay and worried that I would burn in hell. She said, "Don't be a fucking idiot, how do you know you're gay?" I explained my thought process. Mamaw chuckled and seemed to be considering how to explain this to a boy my age. Finally she asked, "J.D., do you want to suck dicks?" I was stunned. Why would anyone want to do that? She repeated herself and I said, "Of course not!" "Then," she said, "you're not gay. And even if you wanted to suck dicks, that would be okay. God would still love you." That settled the matter. Apparently I didn't have to worry about being gay anymore. Now that I'm older, I realize the depth of her sentiment: Gay people, though unfamiliar, did not threaten Mamaw's being. There were more important things for a Christian to be concerned about.

In my new church, on the other hand, I heard more about the gay lobby and the war on Christmas than about any particular character trait a Christian should aspire to. I remembered that moment with Mamaw as an example of secular thinking rather than an act of Christian love. Morality was defined by not participating in this or that social ill: the gay agenda, evolution, Clintonian liberalism, or extramarital sex. Dad's church demanded so little of me. It was easy to be a Christian. The only positive teachings I remember receiving from the church were that I shouldn't cheat on my wife and that I shouldn't be afraid to share the gospel with others. So I planned a life of monogamy and tried to convert other people, even my seventh-grade science teacher, who was a Muslim.

The world was lurching toward moral corruption - toward Gomorrah. The rapture was coming, we thought. Apocalyptic imagery filled weekly sermons and the Left Behind books (one of the best-selling fiction series of all time, which I devoured). People discussed whether the Antichrist was already alive and, if so, which world leader he might be. Someone told me that he expected me to marry a very pretty girl if the Lord hadn't come by the time I reached marriage age. The end times were the natural end for a culture that was sliding so rapidly toward the abyss.

Other writers have noted the terrible retention rates of evangelical churches and blamed this kind of theology for their decline. I didn't appreciate that as a child. Nor did I realize that the religious views I developed during my early years with Dad were sowing the seeds for an outright rejection of the Christian faith. What I did know was that, despite its drawbacks, I loved both my new church and the man who introduced me to it. The timing, as it turned out, was impeccable: The next few months would bring a desperate need for both a heavenly and an earthly father.

Chapter 6

The fall after I turned thirteen, Mom started dating Matt, a younger man who worked as a firefighter. I adored Matt from the start - he was my favorite of all of Mom's men, and we still keep in touch. One night I was home watching TV, waiting for Mom to come home from work with a bucket of KFC for dinner. I had two jobs that night: first, to track down Lindsay in case she was hungry; and second, to run the food over to Mamaw as soon as Mom arrived. Just before I expected Mom, Mamaw called. "Where is your mother?"

"I don't know. What's wrong, Mamaw?"

Her response, more than anything I've ever heard, is seared into my memory. She was worried-frightened, even. The hillbilly accent she usually hid dripped from her lips. "Nobody's seen or heard from Papaw." I told her I'd call as soon as Mama got home, which I expected would be soon.

I thought Mamaw was overreacting. But then I considered the utter predictability of Papaw's schedule. He woke up every day at six am, with no alarm clock, then drove to McDonald's at seven to have coffee with his old Armco buddies. After a few hours of conversation, he would stroll over to Mamaw's house and spend the morning watching TV or playing cards. If he left at all before dinnertime, he might make a quick stop at his friend Paul's hardware store. He always stayed at Mamaw's house to greet me when I came home from school. And if I didn't go to Mamaw's-if I went to Mom's, as I did in good times-he'd usually stop by and say goodbye before he went home for the evening. For him to miss all those events meant something was very wrong.

Mom walked in the door a few minutes after Mamaw called, and I was already sobbing. "Daddy ... Daddy, I think he's dead." The rest is a blur: I think I relayed Mamaw's message; we picked her up down the street and raced over to Papaw's house, which was only a few minutes' drive away. I knocked hard on his door. Mom ran to the back door, screamed, and came around to the front, both to tell Mamaw that he was hunched over in his chair and to grab a rock. She then broke in through a window, unlocked and opened the door, and attended to her father. By then he had been dead almost a day.

Mom and Mamaw sobbed uncontrollably as we waited for the ambulance. I tried to hug Mamaw, but she was beside herself and unresponsive even to me. When she stopped crying, she held me to her chest and told me to say goodbye before they took his body away. I tried, but the medical technician kneeling beside him looked at me as if she thought I was creepy for wanting to look at a dead body. I didn't tell her the real reason I had gone back to my slumped dad.

After the ambulance took Papaw's body away, we went straight to Aunt Wee's house. I guessed Mom had called her because she came down from her porch with tears in her eyes. We all hugged her before squeezing into the car and heading back to Mamaw's. Adults gave me the unenviable task of tracking Lindsay and telling her the news. This was before cell phones, and Lindsay, at seventeen, was hard to reach. She wouldn't answer the house phone, and none of her friends would return my calls. Mamaw's house was literally five doors down from Mom's - 313 McKinley to 303 - so I listened as the adults made plans and watched out the window for signs of my sister's return. The adults talked about funeral arrangements, where Papaw wanted to be buried - "In Jackson, damn it," Mamaw insisted - and who would call Uncle Jimmy and tell him to come home.

Lindsay got home just before midnight. I stomped down the street and opened our door. She walked down the stairs but stopped cold when she saw my face, red and blotchy from crying all day. "Daddy," I blurted. "He's dead." Lindsay collapsed on the stairs and I ran up and hugged her. We sat there for a few minutes, crying like two children do when they find out that the most important man in their lives has died. Lindsay said something then, and although I don't remember the exact phrase, I do remember that Daddy had just done some work on her car, and she mumbled something through the tears about taking advantage of him.

Lindsay was a teenager when Papaw died, at the height of that weird mix of thinking you know everything and caring too much about how others perceive you. Papaw was many things, but he was never cool. He wore the same old T-shirt every day, with a front pocket just big enough to hold a pack of cigarettes. He always smelled of mildew because he washed his clothes but let them dry "naturally," which meant stuffed together in a washing machine. A lifetime of smoking had blessed him with an unlimited supply of phlegm, and he had no problem sharing that phlegm with anyone, no matter the time or occasion. He listened to Johnny Cash on repeat and drove an old El Camino - a car truck - everywhere he went. In other words, Papaw wasn't ideal company for a beautiful seventeen-year-old girl with an active social life. So she took advantage of him the way any young girl takes advantage of a father: She loved and admired him, she asked him for things that he sometimes gave her, and she didn't pay much attention to him when she was with her friends.

To this day, being able to "take advantage" of someone is the measure of having a parent in my mind. For me and Lindsay, the fear of imposition haunted our minds and even infected the food we ate. We instinctively recognized that many of the people we depended on weren't supposed to play that role in our lives, so much so that it was one of the first things Lindsay thought of when she learned of Daddy's death. We were conditioned to feel that we couldn't really depend on people - that even as children, asking someone for a meal or help with a broken-down car was a luxury we shouldn't indulge in too much, lest we fully tap the reservoir of goodwill that serves as a safety valve in our lives. Mamaw and Papaw did everything they could to fight this instinct. On our rare trips to a nice restaurant, they'd interrogate me about what I really wanted until I confessed that, yes, I wanted the steak. And then, over my protests, they'd order it for me. No figure, no matter how imposing, could completely erase that feeling. Papaw had come the closest, but he obviously hadn't made it all the way, and now he was gone.

Papaw died on a Tuesday, and I know this because when Mom's boyfriend, Matt, drove me to a local diner the next morning to pick up food for the whole family, the Lynyrd Skynyrd song "Tuesday's Gone" was playing on the radio. "But somehow I've got to carry on / Tuesday's gone with the wind". That was the moment it really hit me that Daddy was never coming back. The adults did what people do when a loved one dies: They planned a funeral, figured out how to pay for it, and hoped to honor the deceased. We held a visitation in Middletown that Thursday so all the locals could pay their respects, then had a second visitation in Jackson on Friday before the funeral on Saturday. Even in death, Papaw had one foot in Ohio and the other in Holler.

Everyone I cared about came to the funeral in Jackson - Uncle Jimmy and his kids, our extended family and friends, and all the Blanton men who were still kicking. As I looked at these titans of my family, I realized that for the first eleven or so years of my life, I'd seen them at happy times-family reunions and holidays, or lazy summers and long weekends-and for the last two years, I'd only seen them at funerals.

At Papaw's funeral, as at other hillbilly funerals I've attended, the preacher asked everyone to stand and say a few words about the deceased. Sitting next to Uncle Jimmy in the pew, I sobbed through the hour-long service, my eyes so irritated by the end that I could barely see. Still, I knew this was it, and that if I didn't stand up and speak my piece, I would regret it for the rest of my life.

I thought about a moment almost a decade earlier that I'd heard about but couldn't remember. I was four or five years old, sitting in a pew for a great-uncle's funeral at the same Deaton Funeral Home in Jackson. We had just arrived after a long drive from Middletown, and when the minister asked us to bow our heads and pray, I bowed my head and fainted. Mamaw's older brother, Uncle Pet, laid me on my side with a Bible for a pillow and thought nothing of it. I was asleep for what happened next, but I've heard some version of it a hundred times. Even today, when I see someone who was at that funeral, they tell me about my hillbilly Mamaw and Papaw.

When I failed to show up in the crowd of mourners leaving the church, Mamaw and Papaw became suspicious. There were perverts in Jackson, they told me, who wanted to stick sticks up your butt and "blow on your pecker" just as much as the perverts in Ohio or Indiana or California. Daddy hatched a plan: There were only two exits to Deaton's, and no one had left yet. Papaw ran to the car and grabbed a .44 Magnum for himself and a .38 Special for Mamaw. They manned the exits to the funeral home and checked every car. If they met an old friend, they explained the situation and sought help. If they met someone else, they searched the cars like goddamn DEA agents.

Uncle Pet approached, frustrated that Mamaw and Papaw were holding up traffic. When they explained, Pet howled with laughter: "He's asleep in the pew, I'll show you." After they found me, they allowed traffic to flow freely again.

I thought about Daddy buying me a BB gun with a scope attached. He placed the gun on his workbench with a vise to hold it in place and fired repeatedly at a target. After each shot, we adjusted the scope to align the crosshairs with where the BB hit the target. And then he taught me how to shoot-how to focus on the sights, not the target, how to exhale before pulling the trigger. Years later, our Marine boot camp marksmanship instructors would tell us that the kids who already "knew" how to shoot did the worst because they'd learned the wrong fundamentals. This was true with one exception: me. I had learned excellent fundamentals from Papaw, and I qualified with an M16 rifle as an expert, the highest category, with one of the highest scores in my entire platoon.

Papaw was abrasive to the point of absurdity. To any suggestion or behavior he didn't like, Papaw had one response: "Bullshit." That was everyone's cue to shut up. His hobby was cars: he loved buying, trading, and fixing them. One day, not long after Papaw quit drinking, Uncle Jimmy came home to find him fixing an old car in the street. "He was cursing up a storm. Those goddamn Japanese cars, cheap pieces of shit. What a stupid motherfucker who made this thing. I just listened to him, not knowing there was a single person around, and he just kept on complaining. I thought he sounded miserable." Uncle Jimmy had recently started working and was eager to spend his money to help his dad. So he offered to take the car to a mechanic and fix it. The suggestion took Dad completely by surprise. "What? Why?" he asked innocently. "I love fixing cars."

Papaw had a beer gut and a chubby face, but skinny arms and legs. He never said sorry. When he helped Aunt Wee move across the country, she admonished him for his past alcoholism and asked why they rarely had a chance to talk. "Well, talk now. We're in the car together all damn day." But he apologized with actions: The rare times he lost his temper with me were always followed by a new toy or a trip to the ice cream parlor.

Papaw was a terrifying hillbilly made for another time and place. During this cross-country drive with Aunt Wee, they stopped at a highway rest stop in the early morning. Aunt We decided to comb her hair and brush her teeth, spending more time in the ladies' room than Papaw thought wise. He kicked open the door, holding a loaded revolver like a character in a Liam Neeson movie. He was sure, he explained, that she was being raped by a pervert. Years later, after Aunt Wee's dog growled at her baby, Papaw told her husband, Dan, that if he didn't get rid of the dog, Papaw would feed it a steak marinated in antifreeze. He wasn't kidding: Three decades earlier, he had made the same promise to a neighbor after a dog nearly bit my mother. A week later, the dog was dead. At the funeral home, I thought about these things, too.

Mostly I thought about Dad and me. I thought about the hours we spent practicing increasingly complex math problems. He taught me that lack of knowledge and lack of intelligence are not the same. The former could be remedied with a little patience and hard work. And the latter? "Well, I guess you're up the creek without a paddle."

I thought about how Papaw would sit on the floor with me and Aunt Wee's little girls and play with us like a child. Despite his "bullshit" and his grumpiness, he never met a hug or a kiss that he didn't welcome. He bought Lindsay a crappy car and fixed it up, and after she wrecked it, he bought her another one and fixed it up, too, just so she wouldn't feel like she "came from nothing. " "" "" "" I thought about losing my temper with Mom or Lindsay or Mamaw and how those were some of the few times Papaw ever showed a mean streak because, as he once told me, "The measure of a man is how he treats the women in his family. His wisdom came from experience, from his own past failures to treat the women in his family well.

I stood up in that funeral home, determined to tell everyone how important he was. "I never had a father," I explained. "But Papaw was always there for me. He taught me the things men need to know." Then I summed up his impact on my life: "He was the best father anyone could ever ask for.

After the funeral, several people said they appreciated my bravery and courage. Mom was not among them, which struck me as odd. When I found her in the crowd, she seemed to be in a kind of trance: she said little, even to those who approached her. Her movements were slow and her body hunched.

Mamaw also seemed out of sorts. Kentucky was usually the only place she was completely in her element. In Middletown, she could never be herself. At Perkins, our favorite breakfast spot, Mamaw's mouth would sometimes earn her a request from the manager to lower her voice or watch her language. "That son of a bitch," she'd mutter under her breath, chastened and uncomfortable. But at Bill's Family Diner, the only restaurant in Jackson worth sitting down for a meal, she'd yell at the kitchen staff to "hurry the hell up," and they'd laugh and say, "Okay, Bonnie. Then she'd look at me and say, "You know I'm just messing with them, right? You know I'm not a mean old bitch."

In Jackson, among old friends and real hillbillies, she needed no filter. At her brother's funeral a few years earlier, Mamaw and her niece Denise had convinced themselves that one of the pallbearers was a pervert, so they broke into his funeral home office and searched his belongings. They found an extensive magazine collection, including several issues of Beaver Hunt (a magazine that, I assure you, has nothing to do with aquatic mammals). Mamaw thought it was hilarious. "Fucking Beaver Hunt!" she'd yell. "Who comes up with this shit?" She and Denise hatched a plan to take the magazines home and mail them to the pall bearer's wife. After a moment's consideration, she changed her mind. "With my luck," she said, "we'll get in an accident on the way back to Ohio and the police will find these damn things in my trunk. I'll be damned if I'm going out with everyone thinking I'm a lesbian-and a pervert at that!" So they threw the magazines away to "teach that pervert a lesson" and never talked about it again. This side of Mamaw was rarely seen outside Jackson.

Deaton's funeral home in Jackson - where she'd stolen those beaver hunts - was organized like a church. In the center of the building was a main sanctuary flanked by larger rooms with couches and tables. On the other two sides were hallways with exits to a few smaller rooms-offices for the staff, a tiny kitchen, and bathrooms. I've spent much of my life in this tiny funeral home, saying goodbye to aunts and uncles and cousins and great-grandparents. And whether she went to Deaton's to bury an old friend, a brother, or her beloved mother, Mamaw greeted every guest, laughed out loud, and cursed proudly.

So it was a surprise to me when, during Papaw's visitation, I went looking for comfort and found Mamaw alone in a corner of the funeral home, recharging batteries I never knew could be depleted. She was staring blankly at the floor, her fire replaced by something unfamiliar. I knelt before her and laid my head in her lap, saying nothing. That's when I realized Mamaw was not invincible.

In retrospect, it's clear that there was more to Mamaw's and Mom's behavior than grief. Lindsay, Matt, and Mamaw did their best to hide it from me. Mamaw forbade me to stay at Mom's under the guise that Mamaw needed me to be with her while she grieved. Maybe they were hoping to give me some space to grieve for Papaw. I don't know.

At first I didn't see that something had gone wrong. Daddy was dead, and everyone handled it differently. Lindsay spent a lot of time with her friends and was always outgoing. I stayed as close to Mamaw as I could and read the Bible a lot. Mom slept more than usual, and I thought that was her way of coping. At home, she lacked even a modicum of temper control. Lindsay would fail to do the dishes properly or forget to walk the dog, and Mom's anger would erupt: "My dad was the only one who really understood me!" she'd scream. "I've lost him, and you're not making it any easier!" Mom always had a temper, though, so I shrugged it off.

Mom seemed bothered that anyone but her was grieving. Aunt Wee's grief was unwarranted because Mom and Papaw had a special bond. So was Mamaw's, because she didn't even like Papaw and didn't want to live under the same roof. Lindsay and I had to get over it, because it was Mom's father, not ours, who had just died. The first indication that our lives were about to change came one morning when I woke up and walked over to Mom's house, where I knew Lindsay and Mom were sleeping. I went to Lindsay's room first, but she was sleeping in my room instead. I knelt down next to her, woke her up, and she hugged me tightly. After a while she said seriously, "We'll get through this, J" - that was her nickname for me - "I promise. I still don't know why she slept in my room that night, but I would soon learn what she promised we would get through.

A few days after the funeral, I walked out onto Mamaw's porch, looked down the street, and saw an incredible commotion. Mom was standing in her front yard in a bath towel screaming at the only people who really loved her: to Matt, "You're a fucking loser nobody"; to Lindsay, "You're a selfish bitch, he was my dad, not yours, so stop acting like you just lost your dad"; to Tammy, her incredibly sweet friend who was secretly gay, "The only reason you're acting like my friend is because you want to fuck me. I ran over and begged Mom to calm down, but by then a police car was on the scene. I got to the front porch just as a police officer grabbed Mom's shoulders and she collapsed to the ground, kicking and struggling. Then the officer grabbed Mom and carried her to the cruiser, and she struggled all the way. There was blood on the porch and someone said she tried to cut her wrists. I don't think the officer arrested her, although I don't know what happened. Mamaw arrived on the scene and took Lindsay and me with her. I remember thinking if Papaw was here he would know what to do.

Papaw's death shed light on something that had been lurking in the shadows. Only a child could have missed the writing on the wall, I guess. A year earlier, Mom had lost her job at Middletown Hospital after rollerblading through the emergency room. At the time, I saw Mom's bizarre behavior due to her divorce from Bob. Similarly, Mamaw's occasional references to Mom "getting loaded" seemed like random comments from a woman known for her willingness to say anything, not a diagnosis of a deteriorating reality. Not long after Mom lost her job, during my trip to California, I heard from her only once. Little did I know that behind the scenes, the adults - that is, Mamaw on the one hand and Uncle Jimmy and his wife, Aunt Donna, on the other - were debating whether I should move to California permanently.

Mom flailing and screaming in the street was the culmination of things I hadn't seen. She'd started taking prescription narcotics not long after we moved to Preble County. I think the problem started with a legitimate prescription, but soon Mom was stealing from her patients and getting so high that turning an emergency room into a skating rink seemed like a good idea. Papaw's death turned a semi-functioning addict into a woman incapable of following the basic norms of adult behavior.

Thus, Papaw's death permanently changed our family's trajectory. Before his death, I had settled into the chaotic but happy routine of splitting time between Mom and Mamaw. Boyfriends came and went, Mom had good days and bad, but I always had an escape route. With Dad gone and Mom in rehab at the Cincinnati Center for Addiction Treatment-or "the CAT house," as we called it-I began to feel like a burden. Although she never said anything to make me feel unwanted, Mamaw's life had been a constant struggle: From the poverty of the Holler to Papaw's abuse, from Aunt Wee's teenage marriage to Mama's rap sheet, Mamaw had spent the better part of her seven decades managing crises. And now, when most people her age were enjoying the fruits of retirement, she was raising two teenage grandchildren. Without Papaw to help her, that burden seemed twice as heavy. In the months after Papaw's death, I remembered the woman I'd found in an isolated corner of Deaton's funeral home, and I couldn't shake the feeling that no matter what aura of strength Mamaw projected, that other woman lived somewhere inside her.

So instead of retreating to Mamaw's house or calling her every time problems arose with Mom, I relied on Lindsay and myself. Lindsay had just graduated high school and I had just started seventh grade, but we made it work. Sometimes Matt or Tammy would bring us food, but we were mostly on our own: Hamburger Helper, TV dinners, Pop-Tarts, and breakfast cereal. I'm not sure who paid the bills (probably Mamaw). We didn't have much structure-Lindsay once came home from work to find me hanging out with some of her friends, all of us drunk-but in a way, we didn't need it. When Lindsay found out I'd gotten the beer from a friend, she didn't lose her cool or laugh at the indulgence; she kicked everyone out and then lectured me about drug abuse.

We saw Mamaw often, and she asked about us all the time. But we both enjoyed the independence, and I think we enjoyed the feeling that we were no burden to anyone except perhaps each other. Lindsay and I had become so good at crisis management, so emotionally stoic even when the planet itself seemed to be losing its cool, that taking care of ourselves seemed easy. No matter how much we loved Mom, our lives were easier with one less person to care for.

Did we struggle? Sure. We received a letter from the school district informing us that I had accumulated so many unexcused absences that my parents could be called before the school or even prosecuted by the city. We found this letter hilarious: One of my parents had already faced some sort of prosecution and was barely free, while the other was so far off the grid that "summoning" him would require some serious detective work. We also found it frightening: Without a legal guardian around to sign the letter, we didn't know what the hell to do. But as we had done with other challenges, we improvised. Lindsay forged Mom's signature, and the school district stopped sending letters home.

On certain weekdays and weekends, we visited Mom at the CAT house. Between the Kentucky hills, Mamaw and her guns, and Mom's outbursts, I thought I had seen it all. But Mom's latest problem exposed me to the underworld of American addiction. Wednesdays were always devoted to a group activity - a kind of family training. All the addicts and their families sat in a large room, with each family assigned to an individual table, and engaged in a discussion designed to teach us about addiction and its triggers. In one session, Mom explained that she used drugs to escape the stress of paying bills and to numb the pain of Dad's death. In another, Lindsay and I learned that the usual sibling conflict made it difficult for Mom to resist temptation.

These sessions provoked little more than arguments and raw emotions, which I suppose was their purpose. On the nights we sat in that huge hall with other families-all of them either black or white with Southern accents like us-we heard screaming and fighting, children telling their parents they hated them, sobbing parents begging forgiveness in one breath and then blaming their families in the next. It was there that I first heard Lindsay tell Mom how she resented having to play caretaker after Dad died instead of grieving for him, how she hated watching me get attached to one of Mom's boyfriends only to see him walk out on us. Maybe it was the setting, or maybe it was the fact that Lindsay was almost eighteen, but as my sister confronted my mother, I began to see my sister as the real adult. And our routine at home only enhanced her stature.

Mom's rehab progressed quickly, and her condition seemed to improve over time. Sundays were set aside for unstructured family time: We couldn't take Mom out, but we could eat, watch TV, and talk as usual. Sundays were usually happy ones, although on one visit Mom angrily chastised us for getting too close to Mamaw. "I'm your mother, not her," she told us. I realized that Mom had begun to regret the seeds she'd planted with Lindsay and me.

When Mom came home a few months later, she brought a new vocabulary with her. She regularly recited the Serenity Prayer, a staple of addiction circles in which the faithful ask God for the "serenity to accept the things [they] cannot change. Drug addiction was a disease, and just as I wouldn't judge a cancer patient for a tumor, I shouldn't judge a drug addict for her behavior. At thirteen, I found this patently absurd. Mom and I often argued about whether her newfound wisdom was scientific truth or an excuse for people whose choices destroyed a family. Oddly, it's probably both: Research shows a genetic predisposition to drug abuse, but those who believe their addiction is a disease are less likely to fight it. Mom told herself the truth, but the truth did not set her free.

I didn't believe in any of the slogans or sentiments, but I believed she was trying. Addiction treatment seemed to give Mom a sense of purpose, and it gave us something to bond over. I read what I could about her "disease" and even got into the habit of attending some of her Narcotics Anonymous meetings, which were exactly what you'd expect: a depressing conference room, a dozen or so chairs, and a bunch of strangers sitting in a circle introducing themselves as "Bob, and I'm an addict. I thought that if I attended, she might actually get better.

At one meeting, a man arrived minutes late, smelling like a garbage can. His matted hair and dirty clothes spoke of a life on the streets, a truth he confirmed as soon as he opened his mouth. "My kids don't talk to me, nobody does," he told us. "I scrounge up what money I can and spend it on heroin. Tonight I couldn't find any money or heroin, so I came in here because it looked warm." The organizer asked if he'd be willing to try giving up drugs for more than one night, and the man replied with admirable candor: "I could say yes, but honestly, probably not. I'll probably be back tomorrow night."

I never saw the man again. Before he left, someone asked him where he was from. "Well, I've lived here in Hamilton most of my life. But I was born in eastern Kentucky, Owsley County." At the time, I didn't know enough about Kentucky geography to tell the man that he was born no more than twenty miles from my grandparents' childhood home.

Chapter 7

By the time I finished eighth grade, Mom had been sober for at least a year, and she'd been dating Matt for two or three years. I was doing well in school, and Mamaw had taken a couple of vacations-one to California to visit Uncle Jimmy and another to Las Vegas with her friend Kathy. Lindsay had married shortly after Daddy died. I loved her husband, Kevin, and I still do, for one simple reason: He never abused her. That's all I ever wanted in a mate for my sister. Less than a year after her wedding, Lindsay gave birth to her son, Kameron. She was a mother, and a damn good one. I was proud of her and adored my new nephew. Aunt We also had two small children, which gave me three small children to adore. I saw all this as a sign of family renewal. So the summer before high school was hopeful.

That same summer, however, Mom announced that I'd be moving in with Matt at his house in Dayton. I liked Matt, and Mom had lived with him in Dayton for a while. But Dayton was a forty-five minute drive from Mamaw's, and Mom made it clear that she wanted me to go to school in Dayton. I liked my life in Middletown - I wanted to go to high school, I loved my friends, and although it was a bit unconventional, I enjoyed splitting my time between Mom and Mamaw's houses during the week and hanging out with Dad on the weekends. The important thing was that I could always go to Mamaw's house if I needed to, and that made all the difference. I remembered life without that safety valve, and I didn't want to go back to that. Besides, any move would be without Lindsay and Kameron. So when Mom made her announcement about moving in with Matt, I blurted out, "Absolutely not," and stormed out.

Mom concluded from this conversation that I had anger issues and set up a time for me to meet with her therapist. I didn't know she had a therapist or the money to afford one, but I agreed to meet this lady. Our first meeting took place the following week in a musty old office near Dayton, Ohio, where a nondescript middle-aged woman, Mom, and I tried to understand why I was so angry. I realized that people aren't very good at judging themselves: Maybe I was wrong that I was no angrier (in fact, considerably less angry) than most of the people in my life. Maybe Mom was right and I did have some anger issues. I tried to keep an open mind. If nothing else, I thought, this woman might give Mom and me a chance to get things out in the open.

But the first session felt like an ambush. Immediately, the woman began asking why I was yelling at my mother and storming out, why I didn't recognize that she was my mother and that I was legally obligated to live with her. The therapist chronicled "outbursts" I had allegedly had, some dating back to a time I couldn't remember-the time I threw a tantrum in a department store when I was five years old, my fight with another child at school (the school bully, whom I didn't want to hit, but did at Mamaw's encouragement), the times I ran from home to my grandparents' house because of Mom's "discipline. Clearly, this woman had formed an impression of me based solely on what Mom had told her. If I didn't have anger issues before, I have one now.

"Do you have any idea what you're talking about?" I asked. At fourteen, I knew at least a little about professional ethics. "Aren't you supposed to ask me what I think about things and not just criticize me?" I launched into an hour-long summary of my life up to that point. I didn't tell the whole story because I knew I had to choose my words carefully: During Mom's domestic violence case a few years earlier, Lindsay and I had let slip some unsavory details about Mom's parenting, and because it counted as a new revelation of abuse, the family counselor was required to report it to Child Protective Services. So I didn't miss the irony of lying to a therapist (to protect Mom) lest I trigger another intervention by county child services. I explained the situation well enough: After an hour, she simply said, "Maybe we should meet alone."

I saw this woman as an obstacle to be overcome-an obstacle set up by Mom-not as someone who could help. I explained only half of my feelings: that I had no interest in putting a forty-five minute barrier between me and everyone I had ever depended on so that I could get back together with a man I knew would be sent packing. The therapist clearly understood. What I didn't tell her was that for the first time in my life I felt trapped. There was no Papaw, and Mamaw-a longtime smoker with the emphysema to prove it-seemed too frail and exhausted to care for a fourteen-year-old boy. My aunt and uncle had two young children. Lindsay was newly married with her child. I had nowhere to go. I'd seen chaos and fighting, violence, drugs, and a lot of instability. But I never felt I had nowhere to go. When the therapist asked me what I would do, I said I'd probably go live with my dad. She said it seemed like a good idea. As I left her office, I thanked her for her time and knew I'd never see her again.

Mom had a massive blind spot in how she perceived the world. That she would ask me to move to Dayton with her, that she would seem genuinely surprised by my resistance, and that she would subject me to such a one-sided introduction to a therapist meant that Mom didn't understand something about the way Lindsay and I ticked. Lindsay once told me, "Mom just doesn't get it. At first I disagreed with her: "Of course she gets it; it's just the way she is, something she can't change." After the incident with the therapist, I knew Lindsay was right.

Mamaw was unhappy when I told her I wanted to live with Dad, and so was everyone else. No one really understood, and I felt unable to say much about it. I knew that if I told the truth, a few people would offer their spare bedrooms, and everyone would give in to Mamaw's demand that I live with her permanently. I also knew that living with Mamaw would come with a lot of guilt, and a lot of questions about why I wasn't living with my mom or dad, and a lot of people whispering to Mamaw that she just needed to take a break and enjoy her golden years. This feeling of being a burden to Mamaw wasn't something I imagined; it came from a series of little hints, from the things she muttered under her breath, and from the weariness she wore like a dark piece of clothing. I didn't want that, so I chose what seemed like the least bad option.

In a way, I loved living with Dad. His life was normal, just as I'd always wanted mine to be. My stepmother worked part time but was home most of the time. Dad came home from work about the same time every day. One of them (usually my stepmother, but sometimes Dad) would cook dinner every night, which we would eat as a family. Before each meal, we'd say grace (something I'd always liked to do, but had never done outside of Kentucky). On weeknights, we'd watch a family sitcom together. And Dad and Cheryl never yelled at each other. Once I heard them raise their voices during an argument about money, but a slightly raised volume was a far cry from screaming.

On my first weekend at Dad's house - the first weekend I'd ever spent with him when I knew I wasn't going anywhere else come Monday - my younger brother invited a friend to spend the night. We fished in Dad's pond, fed horses, and grilled steaks for dinner. That night we watched Indiana Jones movies until the wee hours. There were no fights, no adults hurling insults at each other, no glass china angrily shattering against the wall or floor. It was a boring evening. And it epitomized what drew me to Dad's house.

What I never lost was the sense of being alert. When I moved in with my father, I'd known him for two years. I knew he was a good man, a little quiet, a devout Christian from a very strict religious tradition. When we first got together, he made it clear that he didn't like my taste in classic rock, especially Led Zeppelin. He wasn't mean about it - that wasn't his style - and he didn't tell me I couldn't listen to the bands I liked; he just advised me to listen to Christian rock instead. I couldn't tell my dad that I played a nerdy collectible card game called Magic for fear he'd think the cards were satanic-after all, kids in the church youth group often talked about Magic and its evil influence on young Christians. And like most teenagers, I had so many questions about my faith-whether it was compatible with modern science, for example, or whether this or that denomination was right about certain doctrinal disputes.

I don't think he would have been upset if I had asked these questions, but I never did because I didn't know how he would react. I didn't know if he would tell me I was a spawn of Satan and send me away. I didn't know how much of our new relationship was based on his feeling that I was a good kid. I didn't know how he would react if I listened to those Zeppelin CDs in his house with my younger siblings around. That not knowing gnawed at me to the point where I could no longer take it.

I think Mamaw understood what was going on in my head, even though I never explicitly told her. We talked a lot on the phone, and one night she told me that I needed to know that she loved me more than anything, and that she wanted me to come home when I was ready. "This is your home, J.D., and it always will be." The next day I called Lindsay and asked her to come get me. She had a job, a house, a husband and a baby. But she said, "I'll be there in forty-five minutes." I apologized to Dad, who was heartbroken by my decision. But he understood: "You can't stay away from your crazy grandmother. I know she's good to you." It was a startling admission from a man to whom Mamaw had never said a kind word. And it was the first indication that Dad understood the complex and conflicting feelings I'd developed. It meant a lot to me. When Lindsay and her family came to pick me up, I got in the car, sighed, and said to her, "Thanks for bringing me home. I kissed my little nephew on the forehead and said nothing else until we got to Mamaw's.

I spent most of the rest of the summer with Mamaw. A few weeks with Dad had not brought me any revelations: I still felt caught between the desire to stay with her and the fear that my presence would deprive her of the comforts of old age. So before my freshman year began, I told Mom that I'd live with her as long as I could stay in the Middletown schools and see Mamaw whenever I wanted. She said something about having to transfer to a Dayton school after my freshman year, but I figured we'd cross that bridge in a year if we had to.

Living with Mom and Matt was like having a front row seat to the end of the world. The fighting was relatively normal by my (and Mom's) standards, but I'm sure poor Matt kept wondering how and when he'd boarded the express train to the crazy town. It was just the three of us in that house, and it was clear to everyone that it wasn't going to work out. It was just a matter of time. Matt was a nice guy, and as Lindsay and I used to joke, nice guys never survived their encounters with our family.

Given the state of Mom and Matt's relationship, I was surprised when I came home from school one day early in my sophomore year and Mom announced that she was getting married. Maybe, I thought, things weren't as bad as I thought. "I really thought you and Matt were going to break up," I said. "You fight every day." "Well," she replied, "I'm not getting married to him."

It was a story that even I found unbelievable. Mom had been working as a nurse at a local dialysis center, a job she'd had for a few months. Her boss, about ten years her senior, asked her out to dinner one night. She accepted, and with her relationship in shambles, she agreed to marry him a week later. She told me on Thursday. We moved into Ken's house that Saturday. This was my fourth home in two years.

Ken was born in Korea but raised by an American veteran and his wife. During that first week at his house, I decided to inspect his small greenhouse and came across a relatively mature marijuana plant. I told Mom, who told Ken, and by the end of the day it had been replaced with a tomato plant. When I confronted Ken, he stammered a bit and finally said, "It's for medicinal purposes, don't worry about it.

Ken's three children-a young girl and two boys about my age-found the new arrangement as strange as I did. The oldest boy fought constantly with Mom, which, thanks to the Appalachian code of honor, meant he fought constantly with me. One night, just before I went to bed, I came downstairs just as he was calling her a bitch. No self-respecting hillbilly could stand idly by, so I made it abundantly clear that I intended to beat my new stepbrother to within an inch of his life. My appetite for violence was so insatiable that night that Mom and Ken decided that my new stepbrother and I should be separated. I wasn't even particularly angry. My desire to fight came more from a sense of duty. But it was a strong sense of duty, so Mom and I went to Mamaw's for the night.

I remember watching an episode of The West Wing about education in America, which the majority of people rightly believe is the key to opportunity. In it, the fictional president debates whether he should push for school vouchers (giving students public money to escape failing public schools) or instead focus exclusively on fixing those same failing schools. This debate is important, of course - for a long time, much of my failing school district qualified for vouchers - but it was striking that in an entire discussion about why poor kids struggle in school, the focus was entirely on public institutions. As a teacher at my old high school told me recently, "They want us to be shepherds for these kids. But nobody wants to talk about the fact that many of them are being raised by wolves.

I don't know what happened the day after Mom and I escaped from Ken's to Mamaw's for the night. Maybe I had a test I couldn't study for. Maybe I had a homework assignment that I never had time to complete. What I do know is that I was a sophomore in high school, and I was miserable. The constant moving and fighting, the seemingly endless carousel of new people I had to meet, learn to love, and then forget, was the real barrier to opportunity, not my inferior public school.

I didn't know it, but I was near the edge. I had almost failed my freshman year of high school with a 2.1 GPA. I didn't do my homework, I didn't study, and my attendance was abysmal. Some days I'd fake being sick, and other days I'd just refuse to go. When I did go, it was only to avoid a repeat of the letters the school had sent home a few years earlier - the ones that said if I didn't go to school, the administration would be forced to refer my case to county social services.

Along with my abysmal school record came drug experimentation-nothing hard, just whatever alcohol I could get my hands on and a stash of weed that Ken's son and I found. Final proof, I suppose, that I knew the difference between a tomato plant and marijuana.

For the first time in my life, I felt disconnected from Lindsay. She'd been married for over a year and had a toddler. There was something heroic about Lindsay's marriage - that after all she'd been through, she'd ended up with someone who treated her well and had a decent job. Lindsay seemed genuinely happy. She was a good mother, doting on her young son. She had a small house not far from Mamaw's and seemed to be finding her way.

Although I was happy for my sister, her new life heightened my sense of separation. We had lived under the same roof all my life, but now she lived in Middletown and I lived with Ken about twenty miles away. While Lindsay was building a life almost antithetical to the one she left behind - she would be a good mother, she would have a successful marriage (and only one) - I found myself mired in the things we both hated. While Lindsay and her new husband took trips to Florida and California, I was stuck in a stranger's house in Miamisburg, Ohio.

Chapter 8

Mamaw knew little about how this arrangement affected me, partly by design. During a long Christmas break, just a few months after I'd moved in with my new stepfather, I called her to complain. But when she answered, I could hear the voices of family in the background - my aunt, I thought, and cousin Gail, and maybe a few others. The background noise suggested holiday merriment, and I didn't have the heart to tell her what I had called to say: that I hated living with these strangers, and that everything that had made my life tolerable up to that point - the reprieve of her house, the company of my sister - seemed to be gone. I asked her to tell everyone whose voice I heard in the background that I loved them, and then I hung up the phone and marched upstairs to watch TV. I had never felt more alone. Fortunately, I continued to attend Middletown schools, which kept me in touch with my school friends and gave me an excuse to spend a few hours with Mamaw. I saw her several times a week during active school sessions, and each time she reminded me of the importance of doing well academically. She often remarked that if anyone in our family was going to "make it," it was going to be me. I didn't have the heart to tell her what was really going on. I was supposed to be a lawyer or a doctor or a businessman, not a high school dropout. But I was closer to dropping out than anything.

She learned the truth when Mom came to me one morning and asked for a jar of clean urine. I had spent the night at Mamaw's and was getting ready for school when Mom came in, frantic and out of breath. She had to submit to random urinalysis by the nursing board to keep her license, and someone had called that morning demanding a sample by the end of the day. Mom's pee was tainted with half a dozen prescription drugs, so I was the only candidate.

Mom's demand came with a strong air of entitlement. She had no remorse, no sense that she was asking me to do anything wrong. There was also no guilt in breaking another promise to never use drugs.

I refused. Sensing my resistance, Mom changed. She became apologetic and distraught. She cried and begged. "I promise I'll be better. I promise." I had heard it many times before, and I didn't believe it one bit. Lindsay once told me that above all else, Mom was a survivor. She survived her childhood, she survived the men who came and went. She survived her many brushes with the law. And now she was doing everything she could to survive a run-in with the nursing board.

I exploded. I told Mom that if she wanted clean piss, she should stop screwing up her life and get it from her own bladder. I told Mamaw that enabling Mom made it worse and that if she'd put her foot down thirty years ago, maybe Mom wouldn't be begging her son for clean piss. I told Mom she was a shitty mother and I told Mamaw she was a shitty mother too. The color drained from Mamaw's face and she refused to even look me in the eye. What I had said had clearly hit a nerve.

Even though I meant those things, I also knew that my urine might not be clean. Mom collapsed on the couch and cried softly, but Mamaw wouldn't give in so easily, even though I had hurt her with my criticism. I pulled Mamaw into the bathroom and whispered a confession-that I had smoked Ken's pot twice in the past few weeks. "I can't give it to her. If Mom takes my pee, we could both be in trouble."

At first, Mamaw allayed my fears. A few pot shots over three weeks wouldn't show up on the screen, she told me. "Besides, you probably didn't know what the hell you were doing. You didn't inhale, even if you tried." Then she addressed the morality of it. "I know it's not right, honey. But she's your mother and she's my daughter. And maybe if we help her this time, she'll finally learn her lesson."

It was the eternal hope, the thing I couldn't say no to. That hope had driven me to volunteer at those many N.A. meetings, to consume books on addiction, and to participate in Mom's treatment as much as I could. It had driven me to get in the car with her when I was twelve, knowing that her emotional state might lead her to do something she'd regret later. Mamaw never lost that hope, after more heartbreak and disappointment than I could possibly fathom. Her life was a clinic in how to lose faith in people, but Mamaw always found a way to believe in the people she loved. So I don't regret giving in. Giving Mom the piss was wrong, but I'll never regret following Mamaw's example. Her hope allowed her to forgive Papaw after the rough years of their marriage. And it convinced her to take me when I needed her most.

Even though I followed Mamaw's example, something inside me broke that morning. I walked to school red-eyes from crying and regretful that I'd helped. A few weeks earlier, I had sat with Mom at a Chinese buffet as she tried in vain to shovel food into her mouth. It's a memory that still makes my blood boil: Mom, unable to open her eyes or close her mouth, spooning food in as it fell back onto the plate. Other people were staring at us, Ken was speechless, and Mom was oblivious. It was a prescription pain pill (or many of them) that had done this to her. I hated her for it and promised myself that if she ever did drugs again, I'd leave the house.

The urine episode was also the last straw for Mamaw. When I came home from school, Mamaw told me she wanted me to live with her permanently, no more moving in and out. Mom did not seem to care: She needed a "break," she said, from being a mother, I suppose. She and Ken didn't last much longer. By the end of sophomore year, she had moved out of his house and I had moved in with Mamaw, never to return to the homes of Mom and her men. At least she passed her pee test.

I didn't even have to pack because much of what I owned stayed with Mamaw as I moved from place to place. She didn't approve of me taking too many of my things to Ken's house, convinced that he and his kids would steal my socks and shirts. (Neither Ken nor his kids ever stole from me.) Although I loved living with her, my new home tested my patience on many levels. I still harbored insecurities that I was a burden to her. More importantly, she was a difficult woman to live with, quick-witted and sharp-tongued. If I didn't take out the garbage, she'd tell me to "stop being a lazy piece of shit. If I forgot to do my homework, she'd call me "shit for brains" and remind me that if I didn't study, I'd be nothing. She demanded that I play card games with her - usually gin rummy - and she never lost. "You're the worst damn card player I ever met," she'd gloat. (That didn't make me feel bad: She said it to everyone she beat, and she beat everyone at gin rummy.)

Years later, every single one of my relatives - Aunt Wee, Uncle Jimmy, even Lindsay - would repeat some version of "Mamaw was really hard on you. Too hard." There were three rules in their house: Get good grades, get a job, and "get off your ass and help me. There was no set list of chores; I just had to help her with whatever she was doing. And she never told me what to do - she'd just yell at me if she was doing something and I wasn't helping.

But we had a lot of fun. Mamaw had a lot more bark than bite, at least with me. She once ordered me to watch a TV show with her on a Friday night, a scary murder mystery, the kind of show Mamaw loved to watch. At the climax of the show, during a moment designed to make the viewer jump, Mamaw turned off the lights and screamed in my ear. She'd seen the episode before and knew what was coming. She made me sit there for forty-five minutes just so she could scare me at the appointed time.

The best thing about living with Mamaw was that I began to understand what made her tick. Until then, I had resented how infrequently we traveled to Kentucky after Mamaw Blanton's death. The decrease in visits wasn't noticeable at first, but by the time I was in middle school, we visited Kentucky only a few times a year for a few days at a time. While living with Mamaw, I learned that she and her sister, Rose - a woman of uncommon kindness - had a falling out after their mother died. Mamaw had hoped that the old house would become a kind of family time-share, while Rose had hoped that the house would go to her son and his family. Rose was right: None of the siblings who lived in Ohio or Indiana visited often enough, so it made sense to give the house to someone who would use it. But Mamaw worried that without a home base, her children and grandchildren would have no place to stay when they visited Jackson. She was right. I began to understand that Mamaw saw returning to Jackson as a duty to be endured rather than a source of pleasure. For me, Jackson was about my uncles and hunting turtles and finding peace from the instability that plagued my existence in Ohio. Jackson gave me a home to share with Mamaw, a three-hour drive to tell and hear stories, and a place where everyone knew me as the grandson of the famous Jim and Bonnie Vance. Jackson was something else to her. It was the place where she sometimes went hungry as a child, where she ran away after a teenage pregnancy scandal, and where so many of her friends had lost their lives in the mines. I wanted to escape to Jackson; she had escaped from it.

In her old age, with limited mobility, Mamaw loved to watch television. She liked bawdy humor and epic dramas, so she had a lot to choose from. But by far her favorite show was HBO's mob saga The Sopranos. Looking back, it's not surprising that a show about fiercely loyal, sometimes violent underdogs resonated with Mamaw. Change the names and the dates, and the Italian Mafia begins to look a lot like the Hatfield-McCoy dispute back in Appalachia. The show's main character, Tony Soprano, was a violent killer, an objectively terrible person by almost any standard. But Mamaw respected his loyalty and the fact that he would do anything to protect his family's honor. Though he murdered countless enemies and drank excessively, the only criticism she ever leveled at him concerned his infidelity. "He always sleeps around. I don't like that."

I also saw for the first time Mamaw's love of children, not as an object of her affection, but as an observer of it. She often babysat for Lindsay's or Aunt Wee's young children. One day she had both of Aunt Wee's girls for the day and Aunt Wee's dog in the backyard. When the dog barked, Mamaw yelled, "Shut up, you son of a bitch. My cousin Bonnie Rose ran to the back door and started yelling over and over, "Son of a bitch! Son of a bitch!" Mamaw hobbled over to Bonnie Rose and scooped her up in her arms. "Shhh! You can't say that, or you'll get me in trouble." But she was laughing so hard she could hardly get the words out. A few weeks later, I came home from school and asked Mamaw how her day had been. She told me she'd had a great day because she'd watched Lindsay's son, Kameron. "He asked me if he could say 'fuck' like me. I told him yes, but only in my house." Then she chuckled to herself. No matter how she was feeling, whether her emphysema was making it hard to breathe or her hip was so bad she could barely walk, she never turned down an opportunity to "spend time with those babies," as she put it. Mamaw loved them, and I began to understand why she had always dreamed of becoming an advocate for abused and neglected children.

At some point, Mamaw underwent major back surgery to relieve the pain that made it difficult to walk. She ended up in a nursing home for a few months to recover, forcing me to live alone, an experience that fortunately didn't last long. Every night she would call Lindsay, Aunt Wee, or me and make the same request: "I hate the damn food here. Can you go to Taco Bell and get me a bean burrito?" In fact, Mamaw hated everything about the nursing home and once asked me to promise that if she ever had to stay there permanently, I'd take my .44 Magnum and put a bullet in her head. "Mamaw, you can't ask me to do that. I'd go to prison for the rest of my life." "Well," she said, pausing for a moment to think, "then get yourself some arsenic. That way no one will know." Her back surgery, it turned out, was completely unnecessary. She had a broken hip, and as soon as a surgeon repaired it, she was back on her feet, though she used a walker or cane from then on. Now that I'm a lawyer, I wonder why we never considered a malpractice suit against the doctor who unnecessarily operated on her back. But Mamaw wouldn't have allowed it: She didn't believe in using the legal system unless you had to.

Sometimes I'd see Mamaw every few days, and sometimes I'd go a few weeks without hearing from her. After a breakup, she spent a few months on Mamaw's couch, and we both enjoyed her company. Mom tried, in her own way: When she worked, she'd always give me money on payday, almost certainly more than she could afford. For reasons I never fully understood, Mom equated money with affection. Perhaps she felt that I would never appreciate that she loved me unless she offered me a wad of pocket money. But I never cared about money. I just wanted her to be well.

Not even my closest friends knew that I was living in my grandmother's house. I realized that while many of my peers lacked the traditional American family, mine was more nontraditional than most. And we were poor, a status Mamaw wore like a badge of honor, but one I'd barely come to terms with. I didn't wear Abercrombie & Fitch or American Eagle unless I got them for Christmas. When Mamaw picked me up from school, I'd ask her not to get out of the car so my friends wouldn't see her in her uniform of baggy jeans and a men's T-shirt with a giant menthol cigarette hanging from her lip. When people asked, I lied and told them that I lived with my mother and that she and I took care of my ailing grandmother. To this day, I regret that far too many high school friends and acquaintances never knew that Mamaw was the best thing that ever happened to me.

My junior year, I enrolled in the honors advanced math class-a hybrid of trigonometry, advanced algebra, and pre-calculus. The class's instructor, Ron Selby, was legendary among the students for his brilliance and high standards. In twenty years, he had never missed a day of school. According to Middletown High School legend, a student called in a bomb threat during one of Selby's exams and hid the device in a bag in his locker. With the entire school evacuated outside, Selby marched into the school, retrieved the contents of the boy's locker, marched outside, and threw the contents into a trash can. "I had that kid in my class; he's not smart enough to make a working bomb," Selby told the police officers gathered at the school. "Now let my students go back to class and finish their exams."

Mamaw loved stories like that, and though she never met Selby, she admired him and encouraged me to follow his example. Selby encouraged (but didn't require) his students to get advanced graphing calculators-the Texas Instruments Model 89 was the latest and greatest. We didn't have cell phones or fancy clothes, but Mamaw made sure I had one of those graphing calculators. This taught me an important lesson about Mamaw's values, and it forced me to care about school in a way I never had before. If Mamaw could drop $180 on a graphing calculator-she insisted that I not spend any of my own money-then I had better take school work more seriously. I owed it to her, and she reminded me of it constantly. "Did you finish your work for that Selby teacher?" "No, Mamaw, not yet." "You damn well better start. I didn't spend every penny I had on that little computer so you could screw around all day."

Those three years with Mamaw - uninterrupted and alone - saved me. I didn't notice the causality of the change, how living with her changed my life. I didn't notice that my grades improved immediately after I moved in. And I couldn't have known that I was making lifelong friends.

During this period, Mamaw and I began to talk about the problems in our community. Mamaw encouraged me to get a job - telling me it would be good for me and that I needed to learn the value of a dollar. When her encouragement fell on deaf ears, she demanded that I get a job, which I did, as a cashier at Dillman's, a local grocery store.

Working as a cashier turned me into an amateur sociologist. A frenetic stress animated so many of our customers. One of our neighbors would come in and yell at me for the smallest transgressions-not smiling at her, or bagging groceries too heavy one day and too light the next. Some came into the store in a hurry, running between the aisles, desperately looking for a particular item. Others waded through the aisles deliberately, carefully checking off each item on their list. Some people bought a lot of canned and frozen foods, while others consistently arrived at the checkout with carts piled high with fresh produce. The more hassled a customer was, the more they bought prepared or frozen foods, the more likely they were to be poor. And I knew they were poor because of the clothes they wore or because they bought their food with food stamps. After a few months, I came home and asked Mamaw why only poor people bought baby food. "Don't rich people have babies?" Mamaw had no answers, and it would be many years before I learned that rich people were significantly more likely to breastfeed their children.

As my job taught me a bit more about America's class divide, it also imbued me with a bit of resentment, directed at both the rich and my own kind. The owners of Dillman's were old-fashioned, so they allowed people with good credit to run food tabs, some of which exceeded a thousand dollars. I knew that if any of my relatives came in and ran up a bill over a thousand dollars, they'd be asked to pay right away. I hated the feeling that my boss thought my people were less trustworthy than those who drove their groceries home in a Cadillac. But I got over it: One day, I said to myself, I'll have my own damn tab. I also learned how people gamed the welfare system. They'd buy two dozen packs of soda with food stamps, then sell them at a discount for cash. They'd ring up their orders separately, buying groceries with food stamps and beer, wine, and cigarettes with cash. They'd regularly walk through the checkout line and talk on their cell phones. I could never understand why our lives felt like a struggle, while those who lived on government largesse enjoyed trinkets I could only dream of.

Mamaw listened intently to my experiences at Dillman's. We began to view many of our fellow working class people with suspicion. Most of us struggled to get by, but we made do, worked hard, and hoped for a better life. But a large minority were content to live on the dole. Every two weeks, I'd get a small paycheck and notice the line where federal and state income taxes were deducted from my paycheck. At least as often, our drug-addicted neighbor would buy T-bone steaks that I was too poor to buy for myself, but Uncle Sam forced me to buy for someone else. That was my seventeen-year-old mindset, and though I'm far less angry now than I was then, it was my first indication that the policies of Mamaw's "party of the working man"- the Democrats-were not all they were cracked up to be.

Political scientists have written millions of words trying to explain how Appalachia and the South went from solidly Democratic to solidly Republican in less than a generation. Some blame race relations and the Democratic Party's embrace of the civil rights movement. Others cite religious faith and the hold that social conservatism has on evangelicals in the region. A large part of the explanation lies in the fact that many in the white working class saw exactly what I was doing working at Dillman's. As early as the 1970s, the white working class began to turn to Richard Nixon because of the perception that, as one man put it, the government was "paying people who are on welfare today to do nothing! They're laughing at our society! And we're all hard-working people, and we get laughed at for working every day!"

About that time, our neighbor - one of Mamaw and Papaw oldest friends - signed up the house next to ours for Section 8. Section 8 is a government program that provides low-income residents with a voucher to rent housing. Mamaw's friend had had little luck renting his property, but by qualifying his house for the Section 8 voucher, he virtually guaranteed that would change. Mamaw saw this as a betrayal that ensured "bad" people would move into the neighborhood and drive down property values.

Despite our efforts to draw bright lines between the working and non-working poor, Mamaw and I realized that we had a lot in common with those we thought were giving our people a bad name. These Section 8 recipients looked a lot like us. The matriarch of the first family to move in next door was born in Kentucky but moved north at a young age when her parents sought a better life. She'd been involved with a couple of men, each of whom had left her with a child but no support. She was nice, and so were her children. But the drugs and the late-night fights revealed problems that too many hillbilly transplants know all too well. Faced with this realization of her own family's struggle, Mamaw became frustrated and angry.

Out of that anger came Bonnie Vance, the social policy expert: "She's a lazy whore, but she wouldn't be if she was forced to get a job"; "I hate those fuckers for giving these people the money to move into our neighborhood. She railed against the people we saw at the grocery store: "I can't understand why people who've worked all their lives are struggling while these deadbeats are using our tax dollars to buy booze and cell phones."

These were bizarre views for my bleeding-heart grandmother. And if one day she'd blame the government for doing too much, the next day she'd blame it for doing too little. After all, the government was just helping poor people find a place to live, and my grandmother loved the idea of anyone helping the poor. She had no philosophical objection to Section 8 vouchers. So the Democrat in her would come out. She would grumble about the lack of jobs and wonder aloud if that was why our neighbor couldn't find a good husband. In her more compassionate moments, Mamaw would ask if it made sense that our society could afford aircraft carriers but not drug treatment facilities like Mom's for everyone. Sometimes she criticized the faceless rich, whom she saw as far too unwilling to pay their fair share of the social burden. Mamaw saw every failure of the local school improvement tax (and there were many) as an indictment of our society's failure to provide a quality education for children like me.

Mamaw's feelings occupied very different parts of the political spectrum. Depending on her mood, Mamaw was either a radical conservative or a European-style social democrat. Because of this, I initially assumed that Mamaw was an unreformed simpleton, and that as soon as she opened her mouth about politics or policy, I might as well close my ears. But I soon realised there was great wisdom in Mamaw's contradictions. I had spent so long just surviving my world, but now that I had a little space to observe it, I began to see the world as Mamaw did. I was scared, confused, angry, and heartbroken. I'd blame big corporations for closing up shop and moving overseas, and then I'd wonder if I could have done the same thing. I'd curse our government for not helping enough, and then I'd wonder if, in its attempts to help, it was actually making the problem worse.

Mamaw could spit venom like a Marine Corps drill instructor, but what she saw in our community didn't just make her mad. It broke her heart. Behind the drugs and the fights and the financial struggles were people with serious problems, and they were hurting. Our neighbors had a kind of desperate sadness in their lives. You'd see it in the way the mother would grin but never really smile, or in the jokes the teenage girl would tell about how her mother "beat the shit out of her. I knew what awkward humor like that was meant to hide because I'd used it in the past. Grin and bear it, the saying goes. If anyone appreciated it, it was Mamaw.

Our community's problems hit close to home. Mamaw's struggles weren't isolated. They were replicated, replayed, and relieved by many who, like us, had moved hundreds of miles in search of a better life. There was no end in sight. Mamaw had thought she had escaped the poverty of the hills, but poverty-emotional if not financial-had followed her. Something had made her later years eerily similar to her earliest years. What was happening? What were the prospects for our neighbor's teenage daughter? Surely the odds were against her with such a home life. This raised the question: What would happen to me? I couldn't answer these questions in a way that didn't implicate something deep within the place I called home. What I did know was that other people didn't live like we did. When I visited Uncle Jimmy, I did not wake up to the neighbors' screams. In Aunt Wee and Dan's neighborhood, the houses were beautiful and the lawns were well-manicured, and the police came around to smile and wave, but never to load someone's mom or dad into the back of their cruiser.

So I wondered what was different about us-not just me and my family, but our neighborhood and our town and everyone from Jackson to Middletown and beyond. When Mom had been arrested a few years earlier, the porches and front yards of the neighborhood had filled with spectators; there's nothing more embarrassing than waving to the neighbors right after the cops have taken your mother away. Mom's exploits were certainly extreme, but we had all seen the show before with different neighbors. These things had their own rhythm. A mild screaming match might invite a few cracked shutters or peering eyes behind the shades. If things escalated a bit, bedrooms would light up as people woke up to investigate the commotion. And if things got out of hand, the police would come and take someone's drunk dad or unhinged mom to the town hall. That building housed the tax collector, the public works department, and even a small museum, but all the kids in my neighborhood knew it as the home of Middletown's short-term jail.

I consumed books on social policy and the working poor. One book in particular, a study by the eminent sociologist William Julius Wilson called The Truly Disadvantaged, struck a chord. I was sixteen when I first read it, and though I didn't fully understand everything, I grasped the central thesis. As millions of people migrated north for factory jobs, the communities that grew up around those factories were vibrant but fragile: when the factories closed their doors, the people left behind were trapped in towns and cities that could no longer support such large populations with quality work. Those who could - generally the well-educated, the wealthy, or the well-connected - left, leaving behind communities of poor people. These remaining people were the "truly disadvantaged"-unable to find good jobs on their own and surrounded by communities that offered little in the way of connections or social support.

Wilson's book spoke to me. I wanted to write him a letter and tell him that he had described my home perfectly. That it resonated so personally is odd, though, because he wasn't writing about Appalachian hillbilly transplants-he was writing about inner-city blacks. The same was true of Charles Murray's groundbreaking Losing Ground, another book about black people that could have been written about hillbillies-it was about the way our government has encouraged social decay through the welfare state.

Though insightful, neither book fully answered the questions that plagued me: Why didn't our neighbor leave her abusive husband? Why was she spending her money on drugs? Why couldn't she see that her behavior was destroying her daughter? Why did all of these things happen not only to our neighbor, but also to my mother? It would be years before I learned that no book, no one expert, no one field could fully explain the problems of hicks in modern America. Our elegy is sociological, yes, but it is also about psychology and community and culture and faith.

During my junior year of high school, our neighbor Pattie called her landlord to report a leaky roof. The landlord arrived to find Pattie topless, stoned, and unconscious on her living room couch. Upstairs, the bathtub was overflowing - hence the leaky roof. Pattie had apparently drawn a bath, taken some prescription painkillers, and passed out. The top floor of her home and many of her family's possessions were destroyed. This is the reality of our fellowship. It's about a naked drug addict destroying what little value there is in her life. It's about children losing their toys and clothes because of a mother's addiction.

Another neighbor lived alone in a large pink house. She was a recluse, an enigma to the neighborhood. She only came out to smoke. She never said hello and her lights were always off. She and her husband had divorced, and her children had ended up in prison. She was extremely obese - as a child I used to wonder if she hated the outdoors because she was too heavy to move.

There were the neighbors down the street, a younger woman with a toddler and her middle-aged boyfriend. The boyfriend worked and the woman spent her days watching The Young and the Restless. Her young son was adorable, and he loved Mamaw. At all hours of the day - once after midnight - he would wander to her doorstep and ask for a snack. His mother had all the time in the world, but she couldn't watch her child closely enough to keep him from wandering into the homes of strangers. Sometimes his diaper had to be changed. Mamaw once called social services, hoping they would somehow rescue the boy. They did nothing. So Mamaw used my nephew's diapers and kept a watchful eye on the neighborhood, always looking for signs of her "little buddy.

My sister's friend lived in a small duplex with her mother (a welfare queen if ever there was one). She had seven siblings, most from the same father - a rarity, unfortunately. Her mother had never held a job and seemed "only interested in breeding," as Mamaw put it. Her children never had a chance. One ended up in an abusive relationship that produced a child before the mother was old enough to buy cigarettes. The oldest overdosed on drugs and was arrested shortly after graduation.

This was my world: a world of truly irrational behavior. We spend ourselves in the poorhouse. We buy huge TVs and iPads. Our kids wear fancy clothes thanks to high-interest credit cards and payday loans. We buy houses we don't need, refinance them for more spending money, and declare bankruptcy, often leaving them full of garbage. Frugality is inimical to our being. We pretend we're upper class. And when the dust settles - when bankruptcy comes or a family member bails us out of our folly - there is nothing left. Nothing for the kids' college tuition, no investments to grow our wealth, no rainy-day fund in case someone loses their job. We know we shouldn't be spending like this. Sometimes we beat ourselves up about it, but we do it anyway.

Our homes are a chaotic mess. We yell and scream at each other like we're spectators at a football game. At least one member of the family is using drugs-sometimes the father, sometimes the mother, sometimes both. At particularly stressful times, we hit and punch each other in front of the rest of the family, including small children; often the neighbors hear what's going on. A bad day is when neighbors call the police to stop the drama. Our children go to foster homes, but never stay long. We apologize to our children. The kids think we're really sorry, and we are. But then we act just as mean a few days later.

We don't study when we are children, and we don't make our children study when we are parents. Our children do poorly in school. We may get angry with them, but we never give them the tools - like peace and quiet at home - to succeed. Even the best and brightest are likely to go to college close to home if they survive the war zone at home. "I don't care if you got into Notre Dame," we say. "You can get a good, cheap education at the community college." The irony is that for poor people like us, a Notre Dame education is both cheaper and finer.

We choose not to work when we should be looking for jobs. Sometimes we get a job, but it doesn't last. We get fired for being late, or for stealing merchandise and selling it on eBay, or for having a customer complain about the smell of alcohol on our breath, or for taking five thirty-minute bathroom breaks per shift. We talk about the value of hard work, but we tell ourselves that the reason we don't work is some perceived injustice: Obama shut down the coal mines, or all the jobs went to the Chinese. These are the lies we tell ourselves to solve the cognitive dissonance-the broken connection between the world we see and the values we preach.

We talk to our children about responsibility, but we never walk the walk. It's like this: For years I'd dreamed of owning a German shepherd puppy. Somehow, Mom found me one. But it was our fourth dog, and I had no idea how to train it. Within a few years, all of them had disappeared-given to the police or to a family friend. After we say goodbye to our fourth dog, our hearts harden. We learn not to get too attached.

Our eating and exercise habits seem designed to send us to an early grave, and it's working: In certain parts of Kentucky, the local life expectancy is sixty-seven, a full decade and a half less than in nearby Virginia. A recent study found that, uniquely among all ethnic groups in the United States, the life expectancy of working-class whites is declining. We eat Pillsbury cinnamon rolls for breakfast, Taco Bell for lunch, and McDonald's for dinner. We rarely cook, even though it's cheaper and better for the body and soul. Exercise is limited to the games we play as children. We only see people jogging in the streets when we leave home for the military or college in a distant place.

Not all of the white working class struggles. I knew as a child that there were two separate sets of mores and social pressures. My grandparents embodied one type: old-fashioned, quietly faithful, self-reliant, hard-working. My mother, and increasingly the whole neighborhood, embodied another: consumerist, isolated, angry, suspicious.

There were (and are) many who live by my grandparents' code. Sometimes you could see it in the most subtle ways: the old neighbor who diligently tended her garden while her neighbors let their houses rot from the inside out; the young woman who grew up with my mother who returned to the neighborhood every day to help her mother navigate old age. I say this not to romanticize my grandparents' way of life-which, I've observed, was fraught with problems-but to note that many in our community may have struggled, but they did so successfully. There are many intact families, many dinners shared in peaceful homes, many children who study hard and believe they'll claim their own American Dream. Many of my friends have built successful lives and happy families in Middletown or nearby. They are not the problem, and if you believe the statistics, the children of these intact homes have much to be optimistic about.

I have always straddled these two worlds. Thanks to Mamaw, I never saw only the worst of what our community had to offer, and I think that saved me. There was always a safe place and a loving embrace if I ever needed it. Our neighbors' children couldn't say the same.

One Sunday, Mamaw agreed to watch Aunt Wee's children for a few hours. Aunt Wee dropped her at ten. I had to work the dreaded eleven to eight shift at the grocery store. I hung out with the kids for about forty-five minutes, then left for work at ten-forty-five. I was unusually upset-even devastated-to leave them. I wanted nothing more than to spend the day with Mamaw and the babies. I told Mamaw this, and instead of telling me to "stop your damn whining," as I expected, she told me she wished I could stay home, too. It was a rare moment of compassion. "But if you want the kind of job where you can spend weekends with your family, you've got to go to college and make something of yourself." This was the essence of Mamaw's genius. She didn't just preach and curse and demand. She showed me what was possible-a peaceful Sunday afternoon with the people I loved-and made sure I knew how to get there.

Reams of social science testify to the positive effects of a loving and stable home. I could cite a dozen studies suggesting that Mamaw's home offered me not just a short-term refuge, but hope for a better life. Whole volumes are devoted to the phenomenon of "resilient children"-children who thrive despite unstable homes because they have the social support of a loving adult.

I know that Mamaw was good for me not because some Harvard psychologist says so, but because I felt it. Consider my life before I moved in with Mamaw. In the middle of the third grade, we left Middletown and my grandparents to live with Bob in Preble County; at the end of the fourth grade, we left Preble County to live in a duplex in Middletown on the 200 block of McKinley Street; at the end of the fifth grade, we left the 200 block of McKinley Street to move to the 300 block of McKinley Street, and by this time Chip was a regular in our house, though he never lived with us; At the end of sixth grade, we stayed on the 300 block of McKinley Street, but Chip had been replaced by Steve (and there were many discussions about moving in with Steve); at the end of seventh grade, Matt had taken Steve's place, Mom was preparing to move in with Matt, and Mom was hoping that I would join her in Dayton; At the end of eighth grade, she demanded that I move to Dayton, and after a brief detour to my dad's house, I agreed; at the end of ninth grade, I moved in with Ken - a complete stranger - and his three kids. On top of that came the drugs, the domestic violence, Child Protective Services snooping into our lives, and Dad's death.

Today, even remembering that time long enough to write it down evokes an intense, indescribable fear in me. Not long ago, I noticed that a Facebook friend (an acquaintance from high school with similarly deep hillbilly roots) was constantly changing boyfriends - in and out of relationships, posting pictures of one guy one week and another three weeks later, fighting on social media with her new fling until the relationship publicly imploded. She's my age with four kids, and when she posted that she'd finally found a man who treated her well (a refrain I'd seen many times before), her thirteen-year-old daughter commented: "Just stop. I just want you and this to stop." I wish I could hug that little girl because I know how she feels. For seven long years I just wanted it to stop. I didn't care about the fighting or the screaming or even the drugs. I just wanted a home, and I wanted to stay there, and I wanted those goddamn strangers to stay the fuck away.

Now consider the sum total of my life after I moved in permanently with Mamaw. At the end of tenth grade, I lived with Mamaw, in her house, with no one else. At the end of eleventh grade, I lived with Mamaw, in her house, with no one else. At the end of twelfth grade, I lived with Mamaw, in her house, with no one else. I could say that the peace of Mamaw's house gave me a safe place to do my homework. I could tell the lack of fighting and instability allowed me to focus on school and my job. I could say that spending all my time in the same house with the same person made it easier for me to make lasting friendships with people at school. I could say that having a job and learning about the world helped me clarify exactly what I wanted out of my own life. In retrospect, these explanations make sense, and I'm sure there is some truth in each of them.

I'm sure a sociologist and a psychologist sitting in a room together could explain why I lost interest in drugs, why my grades improved, why I aced the SAT, and why I found a couple of teachers who inspired me to love learning. But what I remember most is that I was happy - I wasn't afraid of the school bell going off at the end of the day, I knew where I was going to live for the next month, and no one's romantic choices affected my life. And out of that happiness came so many of the opportunities I've had over the past twelve years.

Chapter 9

During my senior year of high school, I tried out for the varsity golf team. I had been taking golf lessons from an old pro for about a year. The summer before senior year, I got a job at a local golf course so I could practice for free. Mamaw never showed any interest in sports, but she encouraged me to learn golf because "it's where rich people do business. Though wise in her own way, Mamaw knew little about the business habits of rich people, and I told her so. "Shut up, you son of a bitch," she told me. "Everybody knows rich people like to golf." But when I practiced my swing in the house (I didn't use a ball, so the only damage I did was to the floor), she demanded that I stop ruining her carpet. "But, Mamaw," I protested sarcastically, "if you don't let me practice, I'll never get to do any business on the golf course. I might as well drop out of high school now and get a job bagging groceries." "You smart ass. If I wasn't crippled, I'd get up right now and knock your head and ass together."

So she helped me pay for my lessons and asked her little brother (my Uncle Gary), the youngest of the Blanton boys, to find me some old clubs. He delivered a nice set of MacGregors, better than anything we could have afforded on our own, and I practiced as much as I could. By the time golf tryouts rolled around, I had enough of a golf swing to keep from embarrassing myself.

I didn't make the team, but I showed enough improvement to justify practicing with my friends who did, and that was all I really wanted. I learned Mamaw was right: Golf was a rich man's game. At the course where I worked, few of our customers came from Middletown's working-class neighborhoods. On my first day of golf practice, I showed up in dress shoes, thinking they were golf shoes. When an enterprising young bully noticed before the first tee that I was wearing a pair of brown Kmart loafers, he taunted me mercilessly for the next four hours. I resisted the urge to bury my putter in his goddamn ear, remembering Mamaw's sage advice to "act like you've been there. (A note on hillbilly loyalty: Reminded of this story recently, Lindsay launched into a tirade about what a loser the kid was. The incident happened thirteen years ago).

I knew in the back of my mind that decisions about my future were coming. All of my friends were planning to go to college; that I had such motivated friends was Mamaw's influence. When I was in seventh grade, many of my neighborhood friends were smoking pot. Mamaw found out and forbade me to see any of them. I realize that most kids ignore such instructions, but most kids don't get them from the likes of Bonnie Vance. She promised that if she saw me in the presence of anyone on the banned list, she would run them over with her car. "No one would ever know," she whispered menacingly.

As my friends headed off to college, I figured I'd do the same. I scored high enough on the SAT to overcome my previous poor grades, and I knew that the only two schools I was interested in attending - Ohio State and Miami University - would both accept me. A few months before graduation, I had decided (admittedly without much thought) to go to Ohio State. A large package arrived in the mail filled with university financial aid information. There was talk of Pell Grants, subsidized loans, unsubsidized loans, scholarships, and something called "work-study. It was all so exciting, if only Mamaw and I could figure out what it all meant. We pored over the forms for hours before concluding that I could buy a decent house in Middletown with the debt I'd incur to go to college. We hadn't actually started the forms yet - that would require another Herculean effort on another day.

Excitement turned to anxiety, but I reminded myself that college was an investment in my future. "It's the only damn thing worth spending money on right now," Mamaw said. She was right, but as I worried less about the financial aid forms, I began to worry for another reason: I wasn't ready. Not all investments are good investments. All this debt, and for what? To get drunk all the time and get terrible grades? Doing well in college required grit, and I had far too little of it.

My high school record left much to be desired: dozens of absences and tardiness, and no school activities to speak of. I was undoubtedly on an upward trajectory, but even toward the end of high school, C's in easy classes revealed a kid unprepared for the rigors of advanced education. At Mamaw's house, I was healing, but as we combed through the financial aid papers, I couldn't shake the feeling that I had a long way to go.

Everything about the unstructured college experience terrified me-from eating healthy food to paying my own bills. I had never done those things. But I knew I wanted more from my life. I knew I wanted to excel in college, get a good job, and give my family the things I'd never had. I just wasn't ready to start that journey. That's when my cousin Rachael-a Marine Corps veteran-advised me to consider the Corps: "They'll whip your ass into shape." Rachael was Uncle Jimmy's oldest daughter and the dean of our generation of grandchildren. All of us, even Lindsay, looked up to Rachael, so her advice carried tremendous weight.

The 9/11 attacks had occurred only a year earlier, during my junior year of high school. Like any self-respecting hick, I considered going to the Middle East to kill terrorists. But the prospect of military service-the screaming drill instructors, the constant training, the separation from my family-frightened me. Until Rachael told me to talk to a recruiter-implicitly arguing that she thought I could handle it-joining the Marines seemed as plausible as flying to Mars. Now, just weeks before I owed Ohio State a tuition deposit, I could think of nothing but the Marine Corps.

So one Saturday in late March, I walked into a military recruiter's office and asked him about the Marine Corps. He didn't try to sell me anything. He told me I'd make very little money, and I might even go to war. "But they'll teach you leadership and turn you into a disciplined young man." This piqued my interest, but the idea of J.D. The U.S. Marine still inspired disbelief. I was a chubby, long-haired kid. When our gym teacher told us to run a mile, I'd walk at least half of it. I'd never gotten up before six a.m. And here was this organization promising that I'd get up regularly at five a.m. and run several miles a day.

I went home and considered my options. I reminded myself that my country needed me and that I would always regret not being in America's newest war. I thought about the GI Bill and how it would help me trade debt for financial freedom. Above all, I knew I had no other choice. It was college or nothing, or the Marines, and I didn't like the first two options. Four years in the Marines, I told myself, would help me become the person I wanted to be. But I didn't want to leave home. Lindsay had just had her second child, a beautiful little girl, and was expecting a third, and my nephew was still a toddler. Lori's kids were babies too. The more I thought about it, the less I wanted to do it. And I knew that if I waited too long, I'd talk myself out of it. So two weeks later, as the Iraq crisis turned into the Iraq War, I signed my name on a dotted line, promising the Marine Corps the first four years of my adult life.

At first, my family scoffed. The Marines weren't for me, and they let me know it. Eventually, knowing I wouldn't change my mind, everyone came around and some even seemed excited. Everyone, that is, except Mamaw. She tried every kind of persuasion: "You're a damn fool; they'll chew you up and spit you out." "Who's going to take care of me?" "You're too dumb for the Marines." "You're too smart for the Marines." "With what's going on in the world, you're going to get your head blown off." "Don't you want to be there for Lindsay's kids?" "I'm worried, and I don't want you to go." Although she came to accept the decision, she never liked it. Just before I left for boot camp, the recruiter came to talk to my frail grandmother. She met him outside, stood up as straight as she could, and glared at him. "Set one foot on my damn porch and I'll blow it off," she advised. "I thought she meant it," he told me later. So they had their talk while he stood in the front yard.

My biggest fear going into boot camp wasn't that I'd get killed in Iraq or that I wouldn't make the cut. I barely worried about those things. But as Mom, Lindsay, and Aunt Wee drove me to the bus that would take me to the airport and from there to boot camp, I imagined my life four years from now. And I saw a world without my grandmother.

Something inside me knew she wouldn't survive my time in the Marines. I wouldn't be coming home, at least not permanently. Home was Middletown with Mamaw in it. And when I was done with the Marines, Mamaw would be gone.

Marine Corps boot camp lasts thirteen weeks, each with a new training focus. The night I arrived at Parris Island, South Carolina, an angry drill instructor greeted my group as we got off the plane. He ordered us onto a bus; after a short ride, another drill instructor ordered us off the bus and onto the famous "yellow footprints. For the next six hours, I was poked and prodded by medical personnel, assigned equipment and uniforms, and lost all my hair. We were allowed one phone call, so of course I called Mamaw and read from the card they gave me: "I arrived safely at Parris Island. I will send my address soon. Goodbye." "Wait, you little bastard. Are you okay?" "Sorry, Mamaw, can't talk. But yes, I'm okay. I'll write as soon as I can." The drill instructor, overhearing my two extra lines of conversation, sarcastically asked if I'd made enough time "for her to tell you a fucking story." That was the first day.

There are no phone calls in boot camp. I was only allowed one, to call Lindsay when her half brother died. It was through letters that I realized how much my family loved me. While most other recruits-that's what they called us; we had to earn the title "Marine" by completing the rigors of boot camp-received a letter every day or two, I sometimes received half a dozen every night. Mamaw wrote every day, sometimes several times, some offering lengthy thoughts on what was wrong with the world, some offering one-sentence streams of consciousness. Mostly, Mamaw wanted to know how my days were going and to reassure me. Recruiters told families that what most of us needed were words of encouragement, and Mamaw delivered in spades. As I struggled with screaming drill instructors and physical fitness routines that pushed my out-of-shape body to its limits, I read every day that Mamaw was proud of me, that she loved me, and that she knew I wouldn't give up. Thanks to either my wisdom or my inherited hoarding tendencies, I have managed to keep almost all of the letters I received from my family.

Many of them shed interesting light on the home I left behind. A letter from Mom asking what I might need and telling me how proud she was of me. "I babysat [Lindsay's children]," she reports. "They were outside playing with snails. They squeezed one and killed it. But I threw it away and told them they didn't do it because Kam got a little upset because he thought he killed it." This is Mom at her best: loving and funny, a woman who delights in her grandchildren. In the same letter, a reference to Greg, probably a boyfriend who has since faded from my memory. And a glimpse into our sense of normalcy: "Mandy's husband Terry," she begins, referring to a friend, "was arrested for parole violation and sent to jail. So they are all okay."

Lindsay also wrote often, sending multiple letters in the same envelope, each on a different piece of paper, with instructions on the back - "Read this one second; this is the last one. Each letter contained a reference to her children. I learned about my oldest niece's successful potty training; my nephew's soccer games; my younger niece's first smile and first attempts to reach for things. After a lifetime of shared triumphs and tragedies, we both loved her children more than anything. Almost every letter I sent home asked her to "kiss the babies and tell them I love them.

Cut off from home and family for the first time, I learned a lot about myself and my culture. Contrary to conventional wisdom, the military is not a landing spot for low-income kids with no other options. The sixty-nine members of my boot camp platoon included black, white, and Hispanic kids; rich kids from upstate New York and poor kids from West Virginia; Catholics, Jews, Protestants, and even a few atheists.

I was naturally drawn to people like myself. "The person I talk to most," I wrote to my family in my first letter home, "is from Leslie County, Kentucky. He talks like he's from Jackson. I told him how much bullshit it is that Catholics get all the free time they do. They get it because of how the church schedule works. He's definitely a country boy because he said, 'What's a Catholic? And I told him it was another form of Christianity. And he said, 'I might have to try that. Mamaw understood exactly where he was coming from. "Down in that part of Kentucky, everybody's a snake handler," she wrote back, only partly joking.

During my time away, Mamaw showed a vulnerability I'd never seen before. Whenever she received a letter from me, she would call my aunt or sister and demand that someone come to her house immediately to interpret my chicken scratches. "I love you a lot and I miss you a lot. I forget you're not here. I think you're coming down the stairs and I can yell at you it's just a feeling you're not really gone. My hands hurt today, the arthritis I guess. . . . I'm going to write more later. I love you, please take care." Mamaw's letters never contained the necessary punctuation and always included a few articles, usually from Reader's Digest, to occupy my time.

She could still be classic Mamaw: mean and fiercely loyal. About a month into my training, I had a nasty exchange with a drill instructor who took me aside for half an hour and forced me to alternate jumping jacks, sit-ups, and short sprints until I was completely exhausted. It was par for the course in boot camp, something almost everyone faced at one time or another. If anything, I was lucky to have avoided it for so long. "Dearest J.D.," Mamaw wrote when she learned of the incident, "I must say I have been waiting for those dick face bastards to start on you - and now they have. There are no words to describe how much they piss me off. ... . . You just keep doing the best you can and keep thinking about that stupid asshole with an IQ of 2 who thinks he is Bobby Badass but he wears girls underwear. I hate them all." When I read this outburst, I thought Mamaw had gotten it all off her chest. But the next day she had more to say: "Hello sweetheart, all I can think about is them dicks yelling at you, that is my job, not them fuckers. Just kidding, I know you'll be whatever you want to be because you're smart, something they're not and they know it. I hate them all. I really hate their guts. Yelling is part of the game they play ... you keep going the best you can and you will come out on top. I had the meanest old hillbilly firmly in my corner, even though she was hundreds of miles away.

At boot camp, mealtime is a marvel of efficiency. You walk through a cafeteria line, holding your tray for the service staff. They dump all the day's offerings on your plate, both because you're afraid to say what you don't like and because you're so hungry you'd eat a dead horse. You sit down, and without looking at your plate (that would be unprofessional) or moving your head (that would also be unprofessional), you shovel food into your mouth until you're told to stop. The whole process takes no more than eight minutes, and if you're not completely full by the end, you're probably suffering from indigestion (which feels about the same).

The only discretionary part of the exercise is dessert, which is served on small plates at the end of the conveyor belt. During the first meal of boot camp, I grabbed the offered piece of cake and marched to my seat. If nothing else tasted good, I figured, this cake must be the exception. Then my drill instructor, a skinny white man with a Tennessee twang, stepped in front of me. He looked me up and down with his small, intense eyes and asked me a question: "You really need that cake, don't you, fat-ass?" I prepared to answer, but the question was obviously rhetorical, because he knocked the cake out of my hands and moved on to his next victim. I never grabbed the pie again. There was an important lesson here, but not one about food or self-control or nutrition. If you'd told me I'd respond to such an insult by cleaning up the cake and returning to my seat, I never would have believed you. The trials of my youth instilled crippling self-doubt. Instead of congratulating myself for overcoming an obstacle, I worried that I'd be overwhelmed by the next. Marine Corps Boot Camp, with its barrage of challenges large and small, began to teach me that I had underestimated myself.

Marine Corps Boot Camp is designed to be a life-defining challenge. From the day you arrive, no one calls you by your name. You're not allowed to say "I" because you're taught to distrust your own individuality. Every question begins with "This recruit" - this recruit needs to use the head (the bathroom); this recruit needs to see the corpsman (the doctor). The few idiots who arrive at boot camp with Marine Corps tattoos are mercilessly scolded. At every turn, recruits are reminded that they are worthless until they complete boot camp and earn the title "Marine. Our platoon started with eighty-three, and by the time we finished, sixty-nine were left. Those who dropped out - mostly for medical reasons - served to reinforce the worthiness of the challenge.

Every time the instructor yelled at me and I stood up proudly; every time I thought I'd fall behind on a run and kept up; every time I learned to do something I thought impossible, like climb the rope, I came a little closer to believing in myself. Psychologists call it "learned helplessness" when a person believes, as I did in my youth, that the choices I make have no effect on the outcomes in my life. From Middletown's world of low expectations to the constant chaos of our home, life had taught me that I had no control. Mamaw and Papaw had kept me from completely succumbing to that notion, and the Marine Corps broke new ground. If I had learned helplessness at home, the Marines taught me learned willfulness.

The day I graduated boot camp was the proudest day of my life. A whole crew of hillbillies showed up for my graduation - eighteen in all - including Mamaw, who sat in a wheelchair, buried under a few blankets, looking more frail than I remembered. I showed everyone around the base, feeling like I had just won the lottery, and when I was released for ten days' leave the next day, we caravanned back to Middletown.

My first day home from boot camp, I walked into my grandfather's old friend's barbershop. Marines are required to keep their hair short, and I wasn't going to slack off just because no one was watching. For the first time, the corner barber - a dying breed, though I didn't know it at the time - greeted me as an adult. I sat in his chair, told a few dirty jokes (most of which I'd only learned a few weeks before), and told a few boot camp stories. When he was about my age, he was drafted into the Army to fight in Korea, so we traded some barbs about the Army and the Marines. After the haircut, he refused to take my money and told me to be safe. He'd cut my hair before, and I'd walked by his shop almost every day for eighteen years. But it was the first time he'd ever shaken my hand and treated me as an equal.

I had many such experiences shortly after boot camp. In those early days as a Marine, all spent in Middletown, every interaction was a revelation. I'd lost forty-five pounds, so many of the people I knew hardly recognized me. My friend Nate, who would later serve as one of my groomsmen, did a double take when I shook his hand at a local mall. Maybe I carried myself a little differently. My old hometown seemed to think so.

The new perspective cuts both ways. Many of the foods I once ate now violated the fitness standards of a Marine. At Mamaw's house, everything was fried - chicken, pickles, tomatoes. The bologna sandwich on toast with crumbled potato chips on the side no longer seemed healthy. Blackberry cobbler, once considered as healthy as any dish based on fruit (blackberries) and grain (flour), lost its luster. I started asking questions I'd never asked before: Is there added sugar? Is this meat high in saturated fat? How much salt? It was just food, but I already knew I'd never look at Middletown the same way again. Within months, the Marine Corps had already changed my perspective.

I soon left home for a permanent assignment in the Marine Corps, and life at home continued apace. I tried to return as often as I could, and with long weekends and generous Marine Corps leave, I usually saw my family every few months. The kids looked a little bigger every time I saw them, and Mom moved in with Mamaw not long after I left for boot camp, though she didn't plan to stay. Mamaw's health seemed to be improving: She was walking better and even gaining a little weight. Lindsay and Aunt Wee and their families were healthy and happy. My greatest fear before I left was that some tragedy would befall my family while I was gone and I wouldn't be able to help. Fortunately, that didn't happen.

In January 2005, I learned that my unit would be deploying to Iraq in a few months. I was both excited and nervous. Mamaw went silent when I called to tell her. After a few uncomfortable seconds of dead air, she said only that she hoped the war would be over before I left. Though we talked on the phone every few days, we never talked about Iraq, even as winter turned to spring and everyone knew I was going to war that summer. I could tell Mamaw didn't want to talk or think about it, and I obliged.

Mamaw was old, frail, and ill. I was no longer living with her, and I was preparing to go to war. Although her health had improved somewhat since I'd left for the Marines, she still took a dozen medications and made quarterly trips to the hospital for various ailments. When AK Steel-which provided Mamaw's health care as Papaw's widow-announced that it was raising her premiums, Mamaw simply couldn't afford them. She was barely surviving, and she needed an extra three hundred dollars a month. She told me this one day, and I immediately volunteered to pay for it. She had never accepted anything from me-no money from my paycheck at Dillman's; no share of my boot camp earnings. But she accepted my three hundred a month, and that's how I knew she was desperate.

I didn't make much money myself - probably a thousand dollars a month after taxes, though the Marines gave me a place to stay and food to eat, so that money went a long way. I also made extra money playing online poker. Poker was in my blood - I had played with pennies and dimes with my dad and great-uncles as far back as I could remember - and the online poker craze at the time made it basically free money. I was playing ten hours a week at low-stakes tables and making four hundred dollars a month. I was going to save that money, but instead I gave it to Mamaw for her health insurance. Mamaw was naturally concerned that I had picked up a gambling habit and was playing cards in a mountain trailer with a bunch of card-sharking hillbillies, but I assured her that it was online and legitimate. "Well, you know, I don't understand the damn Internet. Just don't go for the booze and the women. That's what always happens to fools who get caught up in gambling."

Mamaw and I both loved the movie Terminator 2. We saw it five or six times. Mamaw saw Arnold Schwarzenegger as the embodiment of the American Dream: a strong, capable immigrant making it to the top. But I saw the movie as a kind of metaphor for my own life. Mamaw was my keeper, my protector, and, when necessary, my own goddamn Terminator. No matter what life threw at me, I'd be fine because she was there to protect me.

Paying for her health insurance made me feel like I was the protector for the first time in my life. It gave me a sense of satisfaction I'd never imagined-and how could I? Before the Marines, I'd never had the money to help people. When I got home, I could take Mom out to dinner, get ice cream for the kids, and buy nice Christmas presents for Lindsay. On one of my trips home, Mamaw and I took Lindsay's two oldest kids on a trip to Hocking Hills State Park, a beautiful region of Appalachian Ohio, to meet up with Aunt Wee and Dan. I drove all the way, paid for the gas, and bought everyone dinner (at Wendy's, I admit). I felt like such a man, a real adult. Laughing and joking with the people I love the most as they wolfed down the food I'd provided gave me a sense of joy and accomplishment that words can't possibly describe.

All my life, I had oscillated between fear in my worst moments and a sense of security and stability in my best moments. I was either being hunted by the bad Terminator or protected by the good one. But I had never felt empowered-never believed that I had the ability and responsibility to take care of those I loved. Mamaw could preach about responsibility and hard work, about making something of myself and not making excuses. No pep talk or speech could show me what it felt like to go from seeking protection to providing it. I had to learn that for myself, and once I did, there was no turning back.

Mamaw's seventy-second birthday was April 2005. Just a few weeks before, I was standing in the waiting room of a Walmart Supercenter while auto technicians changed my oil. I called Mamaw on the cell phone I paid for, and she told me about babysitting Lindsay's kids that day. "Meghan is so darn cute," she told me. "I told her to shit in the pot, and for three hours she kept saying 'shit in the pot, shit in the pot, shit in the pot' over and over. I told her to stop or I'd get in trouble, but she never did. I laughed, told Mamaw I loved her, and let her know that her three hundred dollar monthly check was on its way. "J.D., thank you for helping me. I'm very proud of you and I love you."

Two days later, I awoke on a Sunday morning to a phone call from my sister, who said that Mamaw's lung had collapsed, that she was in a coma in the hospital, and that I should come home as soon as possible. Two hours later, I was on my way. I packed my dress blue uniform in case I needed it for a funeral. On the way, a West Virginia state trooper pulled me over for driving ninety-four miles an hour on I-77. He asked why I was in such a hurry, and when I explained, he told me that the highway was free of speed traps for the next seventy miles, after which I would cross into Ohio, and that I should go as fast as I wanted until then. I took my ticket, thanked him profusely, and drove 102 until I crossed the state line. I made the thirteen-hour trip in just under eleven hours.

When I arrived at Middletown Regional Hospital at eleven at night, my entire family was gathered around Mamaw's bed. She was unresponsive, and although her lung had been re-inflated, the infection that had caused it to collapse was showing no signs of responding to treatment. Until that happened, the doctor told us, it would be torture to wake her - if she could be awakened at all.

We waited a few days for signs that the infection was surrendering to the medication. But the signs were the opposite: Her white blood cell count continued to rise, and some of her organs showed signs of severe stress. Her doctor explained that she had no realistic chance of living without a ventilator and feeding tube. We all conferred and decided that if Mamaw's white blood cell count continued to rise after one day, we would pull the plug. Legally, it was Aunt Wee's decision alone, and I'll never forget her tearfully asking me if I thought she was making a mistake. To this day, I'm convinced that she-and we-made the right decision. I guess it's impossible to know for sure. At the time, I wished we had a doctor in the family.

The doctor told us that without the ventilator, Mamaw would die within fifteen minutes, an hour at the most. Instead, she lasted three hours, fighting to the last minute. Everyone was there-Uncle Jimmy, Mom, and Aunt Wee; Lindsay, Kevin, and I-and we gathered around her bed, taking turns whispering in her ear, hoping she heard us. As her heart rate slowed and we realized her time was approaching, I opened a Gideon's Bible to a random passage and began to read. It was First Corinthians, chapter 13, verse 12: "For now we see through a glass, darkly; but then face to face; now I know in part, but then I shall know even as I am known. A few minutes later she died.

I didn't cry when Mamaw died, and I didn't cry for days after. Aunt Wee and Lindsay became frustrated with me, then worried: You're so stoic, they said. You need to grieve like the rest of us or you'll burst.

I was grieving in my own way, but I felt that our whole family was on the verge of collapse, and I wanted to give the impression of emotional strength. We all knew how Mom had reacted to Dad's death, but Mamaw's death created new pressures: It was time to wind up the estate, figure out Mamaw's debts, dispose of her property, and distribute what was left. For the first time, Uncle Jimmy learned about Mom's true financial impact on Mamaw - the cost of drug rehab, the numerous "loans" that were never repaid. To this day, he refuses to speak to her.

For those of us who knew Mamaw's generosity, her financial situation was no surprise. Although Papaw had worked and saved for more than four decades, the only thing of value left was the house he and Mamaw had bought fifty years earlier. And Mamaw's debt was large enough to eat up a significant portion of the home's equity. Fortunately, this was 2005 - the height of the housing bubble. If she had died in 2008, Mamaw's estate probably would have been bankrupt.

In her will, Mamaw divided what was left among her three children, with a twist: Mom's share was split evenly between me and Lindsay. This undoubtedly contributed to Mom's inevitable emotional outburst.

I was so caught up in the financial aspects of Mamaw's death and spending time with relatives I hadn't seen in months that I didn't realize Mom was slowly descending to the same place she had traveled after Papaw's death. But it's hard to miss a freight train barreling toward you, so I noticed soon enough.

Like Papaw, Mamaw wanted a visitation in Middletown so all her friends from Ohio could gather and pay their respects. Like Papaw, she wanted a second visitation and funeral back home in Jackson, at Deaton's. After her funeral, the convoy left for Keck, a holler not far from where Mamaw was born and where our family cemetery is located. In family lore, Keck held an even higher place of honor than Mamaw's birthplace. Her own mother-our beloved Mamaw Blanton-was born in Keck, and Mamaw Blanton's younger sister, Aunt Bonnie, nearly ninety years old herself, owned a beautiful log cabin on the same property. A short hike up the mountain from that log cabin is a relatively flat piece of land that serves as the final resting place for Papaw and Mamaw Blanton and a host of relatives, some born in the nineteenth century. That's where our convoy was headed, through the narrow mountain roads, to deliver Mamaw to the family that had crossed over before her.

I've made this trip with a funeral convoy probably half a dozen times, and every turn reveals a landscape that evokes a memory of a better time. It's impossible to sit in the car for the twenty-minute ride and not exchange stories about the departed, all of which begin with "Remember that time . ?" But after Mamaw's funeral, we didn't recall a string of fond memories about Mamaw and Papaw and Uncle Red and Teaberry and the time Uncle David drove off the side of the mountain, rolled a hundred yards down the hill, and walked away without a scratch. Instead, Lindsay and I listened to Mom tell us that we were too sad, that we loved Mamaw too much, and that Mom had the greater right to grieve because, in her words, "She was my mother, not yours!"

I have never been angry with anyone. I had made excuses for Mom for years. I had tried to help her with her drug problem, read those stupid books about addiction, and taken her to N.A. meetings. I had endured, never complaining, a parade of father figures who all left me feeling empty and distrustful of men. I had agreed to ride in that car with her the day she threatened to kill me, and then I had stood before a judge and lied to him to keep her out of jail. I had moved in with her and Matt, and then with her and Ken, because I wanted her to get better, and I thought if I played along, there was a chance she would. For years, Lindsay called me the "forgiving kid"-the one who saw the best in Mom, the one who made excuses, the one who believed. I opened my mouth to spew pure vitriol in Mom's direction, but Lindsay spoke first: "No, Mom. She was our mom too." That said it all, so I sat quietly.

The day after the funeral, I drove back to North Carolina to rejoin my Marine Corps unit. On the way back, on a narrow mountain road in Virginia, I hit a wet spot coming around a curve and the car began to spin out of control. I was driving fast, and my spinning car showed no signs of slowing down as it hurtled toward the guardrail. I thought for a moment that this was it - that I was going to go over the guardrail and join Mamaw a little sooner than I'd expected - when suddenly the car stopped. It's the closest I've ever come to a truly supernatural event, and though I'm sure some law of friction can explain what happened, I imagined that Mamaw had stopped the car from going over the side of the mountain. I reoriented the car, got back in my lane, and then pulled off to the side. That's when I broke down and let out the tears I'd been holding back for the past two weeks. I spoke to Lindsay and Aunt Wee before resuming my journey, and within a few hours I was back at the base.

My last two years in the Marines flew by and were largely uneventful, but two incidents stand out, each of which speaks to the way the Marine Corps changed my perspective. The first was a moment in Iraq where I was fortunate enough to avoid any real combat, but it still affected me deeply. As a public affairs Marine, I was assigned to different units to get a sense of their daily routines. Sometimes I'd escort civilian press, but usually I'd take photos or write short stories about individual Marines or their work. Early in my deployment, I was assigned to a civil affairs unit to do community outreach. Civil affairs missions were typically considered more dangerous, as a small number of Marines would venture into unprotected Iraqi territory to meet with locals. On our particular mission, senior Marines met with local school officials while the rest of us provided security or hung out with the students, playing soccer and handing out candy and school supplies. One very shy boy came up to me and held out his hand. As I handed him a small eraser, his face lit up with joy for a moment before he ran off to his family, holding his two-cent prize aloft in triumph. I have never seen such excitement on a child's face.

I don't believe in epiphanies. I don't believe in transformative moments, because transformation is harder than a moment. I've seen far too many people overcome with a genuine desire to change, only to lose their nerve when they realize how difficult change really is. But that moment, with that boy, came pretty close for me. All my life I'd been angry at the world. I was angry at my mom and dad, angry that I rode the bus to school while other kids rode with friends, angry that my clothes weren't from Abercrombie, angry that my grandfather died, angry that we lived in a small house. That resentment didn't disappear in an instant, but as I stood there and surveyed the mass of children from a war-torn nation, their school with no running water, and the overjoyed boy, I began to appreciate how lucky I was: born in the greatest country on earth, with every modern convenience at my fingertips, supported by two loving hillbillies, and part of a family that, despite all their quirks, loved me unconditionally. At that moment, I resolved to be the kind of man who would smile if someone gave him an eraser. I didn't quite make it, but without that day in Iraq, I wouldn't be trying.

The other life-changing component of my Marine Corps experience was constant. From the first day, with that scary drill instructor and a piece of cake, to the last, when I grabbed my discharge papers and raced home, the Marine Corps taught me how to live like an adult.

The Marine Corps assumes maximum ignorance from its recruits. It assumes that no one has taught you anything about physical fitness, personal hygiene, or personal finance. I took mandatory classes on balancing a checkbook, saving, and investing. When I came home from boot camp with my fifteen hundred dollars deposited in a mediocre regional bank, a senior enlisted Marine drove me to Navy Federal-a respected credit union-and had me open an account. When I got strep throat and tried to fight it off, my commanding officer noticed and sent me to the doctor.

We used to complain all the time about the biggest perceived difference between our jobs and civilian jobs: In the civilian world, your boss couldn't control your life after you left work. In the Marines, my boss didn't just make sure I did a good job, he made sure I kept my room clean, my hair cut, and my uniforms pressed. He sent an older Marine to supervise me while I shopped for my first car, so I'd end up with a practical car like a Toyota or a Honda, not the BMW I wanted. When I almost agreed to finance this purchase directly through the dealership with a 21 percent interest loan, my chaperone blew a gasket and ordered me to call Navy Fed and get a second quote (it was less than half the interest). I had no idea people did that. Compare banks? I thought they were all the same. Shop around for a loan? I felt so lucky to even get a loan that I was ready to pull the trigger. The Marine Corps required me to think strategically about these decisions, and then it taught me how to do it.

Just as importantly, the Marines changed the expectations I had for myself. In boot camp, the thought of climbing the thirty-foot rope was terrifying; by the end of my first year, I could climb the rope with only one arm. Before enlisting, I had never run a continuous mile. On my last fitness test, I ran three of them in nineteen minutes. It was in the Marine Corps where I first ordered grown men to do a job and watched them listen; where I learned that leadership depends far more on earning the respect of your subordinates than on bossing them around; where I discovered how to earn that respect; and where I saw that men and women of different social classes and races could work as a team and bond like a family. It was the Marine Corps that first gave me the opportunity to truly fail, let me take that chance, and then, when I failed, gave me another chance anyway.

When you work in public affairs, the most senior Marines serve as liaisons to the press. The press is the holy grail of Marine Corps public affairs: the biggest audience and the highest stakes. Our media officer at Cherry Point was a captain who, for reasons I never understood, quickly fell out of favor with the base brass. Even though he was a captain - eight pay grades above me - there was no ready replacement when he got the ax because of the wars in Iraq and Afghanistan. So my boss told me that for the next nine months (until my service ended), I would be the media relations officer for one of the largest military bases on the East Coast.

By then, I'd gotten used to the sometimes random nature of Marine Corps assignments. This was very different. As a friend joked, I had a face for radio and wasn't prepared for live TV interviews about what was going on at the base. The Marine Corps threw me to the wolves. I struggled a bit at first-allowing some photographers to take pictures of a classified aircraft; speaking out of turn at a meeting with senior officers-and I got my ass kicked. My boss, Shawn Haney, explained what I needed to do to correct myself. We discussed how to build relationships with the press, how to stay on message, and how to manage my time. I got better, and when hundreds of thousands of people flocked to our base for a semi-annual air show, our media relations worked so well that I earned a commendation medal.

The experience taught me a valuable lesson: that I could do this. I could work twenty-hour days if I had to. I could speak clearly and confidently with TV cameras in my face. I could stand in a room with majors, colonels, and generals and hold my own. I could do a captain's job, even when I feared I couldn't.

For all my grandmother's efforts, for all her "You can do anything; don't be like those fuckers who think the deck is stacked against them" diatribes, the message had only partially sunk in before I enlisted. Surrounding me was another message: that I and people like me weren't good enough; that the reason Middletown produced zero Ivy League graduates was some genetic or character defect. I couldn't possibly see how destructive this mentality was until I escaped it. The Marine Corps replaced it with something else, something that abhors excuses. "Giving it my all" was a catchphrase, something you heard in health or physical education class. The first time I ran three miles, mildly impressed with my mediocre twenty-five-minute time, a terrifying senior drill instructor greeted me at the finish line: "If you're not puking, you're lazy! Stop being fucking lazy!" He then ordered me to sprint repeatedly between him and a tree. Just when I thought I was going to faint, he stopped. I was heaving, barely able to catch my breath. "That's how you should feel at the end of every run!" he yelled. In the Marines, going all out was a way of life.

I'm not saying skill doesn't matter. It certainly helps. But there's something powerful about realizing that you've underestimated yourself - that somehow your mind has confused lack of effort with inability. That's why when people ask me what I'd most like to change about the white working class, I say, "The feeling that our choices don't matter. The Marine Corps removed that feeling like a surgeon removes a tumor.

A few days after my twenty-third birthday, I hopped into the first big purchase I'd ever made - an old Honda Civic - grabbed my discharge papers, and drove one last time from Cherry Point, North Carolina, to Middletown, Ohio. During my four years in the Marines, I had seen a poverty level in Haiti that I had never known. I had witnessed the fiery aftermath of a plane crash into a residential neighborhood. I had seen Mamaw die and then go to war a few months later. I had befriended a former crack dealer who turned out to be the hardest working Marine I knew.

When I joined the Marine Corps, I did so in part because I wasn't ready for adulthood. I didn't know how to balance a checkbook, let alone fill out financial aid forms for college. Now I knew exactly what I wanted out of life and how to get there. And in three weeks, I'd be starting classes at Ohio State.

Chapter 10

I arrived at Ohio State for orientation in early September 2007, and I couldn't have been more excited. I remember every little detail of that day: lunch at Chipotle, the first time Lindsay had ever eaten there; the walk from the orientation building to the South Campus house that would soon be my home in Columbus; the beautiful weather. I met with a guidance counselor who talked me through my first college schedule, which had me in class only four days a week, never before nine thirty in the morning. After the Marine Corps and its five-thirty wake-up calls, I couldn't believe my luck.

Ohio State's main campus in Columbus is about a hundred miles from Middletown, which meant it was close enough for weekend visits with my family. For the first time in years, I was able to visit Middletown whenever I felt like it. And while Havelock (the North Carolina city closest to my Marine Corps base) was not too different from Middletown, Columbus felt like an urban paradise. It was (and still is) one of the fastest growing cities in the country, fueled in large part by the vibrant university that was now my home. OSU grads were starting businesses, historic buildings were being converted into new restaurants and bars, and even the worst neighborhoods seemed to be undergoing significant revitalization. Not long after I moved to Columbus, one of my best friends started working as a promotions director for a local radio station, so I always knew what was going on around town and had access to the city's best events, from local festivals to VIP seats at the annual fireworks show.

In many ways, college was very familiar. I made many new friends, but virtually all were from southwest Ohio. My six roommates included five Middletown High School graduates and one graduate of Edgewood High School in nearby Trenton. They were a little younger (the Marine Corps had aged me past the age of the typical college freshman), but I knew most of them from back home. My closest friends had graduated or were about to graduate, but many stayed in

Columbus after graduation. Though I didn't know it, I was witnessing a phenomenon that social scientists call "brain drain"-people who can leave struggling cities often do, and when they find a new home with educational and job opportunities, they stay. Years later, I looked at my wedding party of six groomsmen and realized that every single one of them, like me, had grown up in a small town in Ohio before going to Ohio State. To a man, they had all found careers outside of their hometowns, and none of them had any interest in ever moving back.

When I got to Ohio State, the Marine Corps had given me an incredible sense of invincibility. I'd go to class, do my homework, study in the library, and make it home in time to drink well past midnight with my buddies, then wake up early to go running. My schedule was intense, but everything that had made me dread independent college life when I was eighteen now felt like a cakewalk. A few years earlier, I had waded through those financial aid forms with Mamaw, arguing over whether to list her or Mom as my "parent/guardian. We had feared that if I didn't somehow obtain and submit Bob Hamel's (my legal father's) financial information, I would be guilty of fraud. The whole experience had made us both painfully aware of how out of touch we were with the outside world. I had nearly flunked out of high school, earning Ds and Fs in English I. Now I was paying my own bills and earning A's in every class I took at my state's flagship university. I felt in control of my destiny in a way I never had before.

I knew Ohio State was a make-or-break time. I had left the Marine Corps not only with a sense that I could do what I wanted, but with the ability to plan. I wanted to go to law school, and I knew that to get into the best law school, I'd have to get good grades and ace the infamous Law School Admissions Test, or LSAT. Of course, there was a lot I didn't know. I couldn't really explain why I wanted to go to law school, other than the fact that the "rich kids" in Middletown were either born to doctors or lawyers, and I didn't want to work with blood. I didn't know how much else was out there, but the little knowledge I had at least gave me direction, and that was all I needed.

I loathed debt and the sense of limitation it imposed. Although the GI Bill paid for a significant portion of my education, and Ohio State charged relatively little for an in-state resident, I still had about twenty thousand dollars in expenses to cover on my own. I took a job at the Ohio Statehouse, working for a remarkably nice senator from the Cincinnati area named Bob Schuler. He was a good man, and I liked his policies, so when constituents called and complained, I tried to explain his positions. I watched lobbyists come and go and listened as the senator and his staff debated whether a particular bill was good for his constituents, good for his state, or good for both. Observing the political process from the inside made me appreciate it in a way that watching cable news never did. Mamaw had thought that all politicians were crooks, but I learned that at the Ohio Statehouse that was largely untrue, regardless of their politics.

After a few months in the Ohio Senate, as my bills piled up and I found fewer and fewer ways to make up the difference between my expenses and my income (you can only donate plasma twice a week, I learned), I decided to get another job. A nonprofit organization advertised a part-time job that paid ten dollars an hour, but when I showed up for the interview wearing khakis, an ugly lime-green shirt, and Marine Corps combat boots (my only non-sneakers at the time) and saw the interviewer's reaction, I knew I was out of luck. I barely noticed the rejection email a week later. A local nonprofit that worked with abused and neglected children also paid ten dollars an hour, so I went to Target, bought a nicer shirt and a pair of black shoes, and came away with a job offer as a "consultant. Their mission was important to me, and they were great people. I started working immediately.

With two jobs and a full-time course load, my schedule intensified, but I didn't mind. I didn't realize there was anything unusual about my commitments until a professor emailed me about meeting after class to discuss a writing assignment. When I sent him my schedule, he was appalled. He sternly told me to focus on my education and not let work distractions get in the way. I smiled, shook his hand, and thanked him. I did not heed his advice. I liked staying up late to work on assignments, waking up early after only three or four hours of sleep, and patting myself on the back for being able to do it. After so many years of fearing my own future, worrying that I would end up like so many of my neighbors or family - addicted to drugs or alcohol, in jail, or with children I couldn't or wouldn't take care of - I felt incredible momentum. I knew the statistics. I had read the pamphlets in the social worker's office when I was a kid. I had seen the look of pity from the hygienist at the low-income dental clinic. I wasn't supposed to make it, but I was doing fine on my own.

Did I go too far? Absolutely. I didn't get enough sleep. I drank too much and ate Taco Bell for almost every meal. A week into what I thought was just a really bad cold, a doctor told me I had mono. I ignored him and continued to live as if NyQuil and DayQuil were magical elixirs. After a week, my urine turned a disgusting brown and my temperature was 103. I realized I needed to take care of myself, so I took some Tylenol, drank a couple of beers, and went to sleep.

When Mom found out what happened, she drove to Columbus and took me to the emergency room. She wasn't perfect, she wasn't even a practicing nurse, but she took pride in overseeing every interaction we had with the health care system. She asked the right questions, got annoyed with doctors when they didn't answer directly, and made sure I had what I needed. I spent two full days in the hospital as the doctors emptied five bags of saline to rehydrate me and discovered that I had contracted a staph infection in addition to the mono, which explained why I was getting so sick. Doctors released me to my mother, who wheeled me out of the hospital and took me home to recover.

My illness lasted a few more weeks, which fortunately coincided with the break between spring and summer semesters at Ohio State. While in Middletown, I split my time between Aunt Wee's and Mom's; both took care of me and treated me like a son. It was my first real introduction to the competing emotional demands of Middletown in a post-Mamaw world: I didn't want to hurt Mom's feelings, but the past had created rifts that would probably never heal. I never faced those demands head-on. I never explained to Mom that no matter how kind and caring she was at any given time-and while I had mono, she couldn't have been a better mother-I just didn't feel comfortable around her. Sleeping in her house meant talking to husband number five, a kind man but a stranger who would never be anything to me but the future ex-Mr. Mom. It meant looking at her furniture and remembering the time I hid behind it during one of her fights with Bob. It meant trying to understand how Mom could be such a contradiction-a woman who sat patiently with me for days in the hospital, and an addict who would lie to her family a month later to get money from them.

I knew my increasingly close relationship with Aunt Wee hurt Mom's feelings. She talked about it all the time. "I'm your mother, not her," she would repeat. To this day, I often wonder if I'd had the courage as an adult that I had as a child, Mom might have gotten better. Addicts are at their weakest during emotionally difficult times, and I knew I had the power to save her from at least some of the sadness. But I couldn't do it anymore. I didn't know what had changed, but I wasn't that person anymore. Maybe it was just self-preservation. Regardless, I couldn't pretend to feel at home with her.

After a few weeks of mono, I felt well enough to return to Columbus and my classes. I'd lost a lot of weight-twenty pounds in four weeks-but otherwise I felt pretty good. With the hospital bills piling up, I got a third job (as an SAT tutor at the Princeton Review) that paid an incredible eighteen dollars an hour. Three jobs was too much, so I quit the job I loved the most - my work in the Ohio Senate - because it paid the least. I needed money and the financial freedom it provided, not rewarding work. That, I told myself, would come later.

Shortly before I left, the Ohio Senate debated a measure that would significantly curtail payday lending practices. My senator opposed the bill (one of the few senators who did), and though he never explained why, I liked to think that maybe he and I had something in common. The senators and policy staff who debated the bill had little appreciation for the role of payday lenders in the underground economy that people like me occupied. To them, payday lenders were predatory sharks who charged high interest rates on loans and exorbitant fees for cashing checks. The sooner they are wiped, the better.

For me, payday lenders could solve important financial problems. My credit was terrible, thanks to a series of terrible financial decisions (some of which weren't my fault, but many of which were), so credit cards were out of the question. If I wanted to take a girl out to dinner or needed a book for school and had no money in the bank, I didn't have many options. (I probably could have asked my aunt or uncle, but I really wanted to do things on my own). One Friday morning, I dropped off my rent check, knowing that if I waited another day, the fifty-dollar late fee would kick in. I didn't have enough money to cover the check, but I would get paid that day and could deposit the money after work. However, after a long day at the Senate, I forgot to pick up my paycheck before I left. By the time I realized the mistake, I was home and the Statehouse staff had left for the weekend. That day, a three-day payday loan with a few dollars in interest allowed me to avoid a substantial overdraft fee. Lawmakers debating the merits of payday lending didn't mention situations like this. The lesson? Powerful people sometimes do things to help people like me without really understanding people like me.

My second year of college started out pretty much the same as my first, with a beautiful day and a lot of excitement. I was a little busier with the new job, but I didn't mind the work. What I did mind was the nagging feeling that, at twenty-four, I was a little too old to be a sophomore in college. But with four years in the Marine Corps behind me, more than age separated me from the other students. During an undergraduate seminar on foreign policy, I listened to a nineteen-year-old classmate with a hideous beard rant about the war in Iraq. He explained that those fighting the war tended to be less intelligent than those (like him) who went straight to college. It showed, he argued, in the wanton way soldiers slaughtered and disrespected Iraqi civilians. It was an objectively terrible opinion - my Marine Corps friends spanned the political spectrum and held almost every conceivable opinion about the war. Many of my Marine Corps friends were staunch liberals who had no love for our commander in chief - then George W. Bush - and felt that we had sacrificed too much for too little. But none of them had ever uttered such unthinking nonsense.

As the student chatted, I thought about the endless training on how to respect Iraqi culture-never show the bottom of your foot to anyone, never speak to a woman in traditional Muslim dress without first speaking to a male relative. I thought about the security we provided for Iraqi election workers, and how we carefully explained the importance of their mission without ever imposing our own political views on them. I thought about listening to a young Iraqi (who didn't speak a word of English) flawlessly rap every single word of 50 Cent's "In Da Club" and laughing with him and his friends. I thought about my friends who were covered in third-degree burns, "lucky" to have survived an IED attack in the Al-Qaim region of Iraq. And here was this idiot with a spotty beard telling our class that we murdered people for sport.

I immediately felt an urge to finish college as soon as possible. I met with a guidance counselor and plotted my exit - I would have to take classes over the summer and more than double the full-time course load during some semesters. It was an intense year, even by my heightened standards. During a particularly awful February, I sat down with my calendar and counted the number of days since I'd slept more than four hours in a day. The number was thirty-nine. But I kept going, and in August 2009, after one year and eleven months at Ohio State, I graduated summa cum laude with a double major. I tried to skip graduation, but my family wouldn't let me. So I sat in an uncomfortable chair for three hours before I walked across the stage and received my college diploma. When Gordon Gee, then president of Ohio State University, paused for an unusually long photo with the girl in line before me, I extended my hand to his assistant and nonverbally asked for the diploma. She handed it to me, and I stepped behind Dr. Gee and off the podium. I may have been the only graduate that day who did not shake his hand. Next, I thought.

I knew I wasn't going to law school until the following year (my August graduation prevented me from starting law school in 2009), so I moved home to save money. Aunt Wee had taken Mamaw's place as family matriarch: She put out the fires, hosted family gatherings, and kept us all from falling apart. She had always provided a home base for me after Mamaw's death, but ten months seemed like an imposition; I didn't like the idea of disrupting her family's routine. But she insisted, "J.D., this is your home now. It's the only place you can stay."

Those last months in Middletown were the happiest of my life. I was finally a college graduate, and I knew I'd soon be fulfilling another dream - going to law school. I worked odd jobs to save money and became close to my aunt's two daughters. Every day I'd come home from work, dusty and sweaty from manual labor, and sit at the dinner table listening to my teenage cousins talk about their days at school and their trials with friends. Sometimes I'd help with homework. On Fridays during Lent, I helped with the fish fry at the local Catholic church. The feeling I had in college-that I had survived decades of chaos and heartbreak and had finally come out the other side-deepened.

The incredible optimism I felt about my own life was in stark contrast to the pessimism of so many of my neighbors. Years of decline in the blue-collar economy were manifesting themselves in the material prospects of Middletown residents. The Great Recession and the not-so-great recovery that followed had accelerated Middletown's downward spiral. But there was something almost spiritual about the cynicism of the community at large, something that went much deeper than a short-term recession.

As a culture, we had no heroes. Certainly no politician-Barack Obama was then (and probably still is) the most admired man in America, but even as the country was enthralled by his rise, most Middletonians viewed him with suspicion. George W. Bush had few fans in 2008. Many loved Bill Clinton, but many more saw him as a symbol of American moral decay, and Ronald Reagan was long dead. We loved the military, but there was no George S. Patton figure in the modern army. I doubt my neighbors could even name a senior military officer. The space program, long a source of pride, had gone the way of the dodo, and with it the celebrity astronauts. Nothing connected us to the core fabric of American society. We felt trapped in two seemingly unwinnable wars, in which a disproportionate number of the fighters were from our neighborhoods, and in an economy that failed to deliver the most basic promise of the American dream-a steady paycheck.

To understand the significance of this cultural disconnect, you have to understand that much of the identity of my family, my neighborhood, and my community comes from our love of country. I couldn't tell you anything about Breathitt County's mayor, its health services, or its famous residents. But I do know this: "Bloody Breathitt" supposedly got its name because the county filled its World War I draft quota entirely with volunteers - the only county in the entire United States to do so. Nearly a century later, that's the Breathitt fact I remember best: It's the truth that everyone around me made sure I knew. I once interviewed Mamaw for a World War II class project. After seventy years of marriage, children, grandchildren, death, poverty, and triumph, Mamaw was undoubtedly proudest and most excited about the fact that she and her family had done their part in World War II. We talked for minutes about everything else; we talked for hours about war rations, Rosie the Riveter, her father's wartime love letters to her mother from the Pacific, and the day "we dropped the bomb. Mamaw always had two gods: Jesus Christ and the United States of America. I was no different, nor was anyone else I knew.

I'm the kind of patriot people laugh at on the Acela corridor. I choke when I hear Lee Greenwood's cheesy anthem, "Proud to Be an American." When I was sixteen, I vowed that every time I met a veteran, I would go out of my way to shake his or her hand, even if it meant awkwardly interrupting them. To this day, I refuse to watch Saving Private Ryan with anyone but my closest friends because I can't stop crying during the final scene.

Mamaw and Papaw taught me we live in the best and greatest country in the world. This fact gave meaning to my childhood. Whenever times were hard - when I felt overwhelmed by the drama and turmoil of my youth - I knew that better days were ahead because I lived in a country that allowed me to make the good choices that others didn't. Today, when I think about my life and how truly incredible it is-a beautiful, kind, brilliant life partner; the financial security I dreamed of as a child; great friends and exciting new experiences-I feel an overwhelming appreciation for this United States. I know it's corny, but that's how I feel.

If Mamaw's second god was the United States of America, then many people in my community were losing something like a religion. The bond that bound them to their neighbors, that inspired them the way my patriotism had always inspired me, had seemingly vanished.

The symptoms are all around us. Significant percentages of white conservative voters - about a third - believe Barack Obama is Muslim. In one poll, 32 percent of conservatives said they believed Obama was foreign-born, and another 19 percent said they weren't sure - meaning that a majority of white conservatives aren't even sure Obama is an American. I regularly hear from acquaintances or distant family members that Obama has ties to Islamic extremists, is a traitor, or was born in some faraway corner of the world.

Many of my new friends blame racism for this perception of the president. But the president feels like an alien to many Middletonians for reasons that have nothing to do with skin color. Consider that none of my high school classmates attended an Ivy League school. Barack Obama attended two of them and excelled at both. He is brilliant, wealthy, and speaks like a constitutional law professor-which, of course, he is. Nothing about him resembles the people I admired growing up: His accent-clean, perfect, neutral-is foreign; his credentials are so impressive they're frightening; he made his life in Chicago, a dense metropolis; and he carries himself with a confidence that comes from knowing that the modern American meritocracy was built for him. Of course, Obama overcame adversity in his own right

- adversity familiar to many of us - but that was long before any of us knew him.

President Obama arrived on the scene just as so many people in my community were beginning to believe that the modern American meritocracy was not built for them. We know we're not doing well. We see it every day: in the obituaries for teenagers that conspicuously omit the cause of death (read between the lines: overdose), in the deadbeats we watch our daughters waste their time with. Barack Obama strikes at the heart of our deepest insecurities. He's a good father when many of us aren't. He wears suits to work, while we wear overalls, if we're lucky enough to have jobs at all. His wife tells us not to feed our children certain foods, and we hate her for it-not because we think she's wrong, but because we know she's right.

Many try to blame the anger and cynicism of working-class whites on misinformation. Granted, there is an industry of conspiracy theorists and fringe lunatics writing about all sorts of idiocy, from Obama's alleged religious leanings to his ancestry. But every major news organization, even the oft-maligned Fox News, has always told the truth about Obama's citizenship status and religious views. The people I know are well aware of what the major news organizations have to say on the subject; they just don't believe them. Only 6 percent of American voters believe the media is "very trustworthy." For many of us, the free press-that bulwark of American democracy-is simply full of shit.

With little trust in the press, there's no check on the Internet conspiracy theories that dominate the digital world. Barack Obama is an alien who is actively trying to destroy our country. Everything the media tells us is a lie. Many in the white working class believe the worst about their society. Here's a small sample of emails or messages I've seen from friends or family:

- •From right-wing radio talker Alex Jones on the ten-year anniversary of 9/11, a documentary about the "unanswered question" of the terrorist attacks, suggesting that the U.S. government played a role in the massacre of its own people.

- •From an email chain, a story that the Obamacare legislation requires microchip implantation in new health care patients. This story carries extra bite because of the religious implications: Many believe that the End Times "mark of the beast" foretold in biblical prophecy will be an electronic device. Multiple friends warned others about this threat via social media.
- •From the popular website WorldNetDaily, an editorial suggesting that the Newtown gun massacre was engineered by the federal government to turn public opinion on gun control measures.
- •From multiple Internet sources, suggestions that Obama will soon implement martial law to secure power for a third presidential term.

The list goes on. It's impossible to know how many people believe one or more of these stories. But if a third of our community questions the president's heritage-despite all the evidence to the contrary-it's a good bet that the other conspiracies have more currency than we'd like. This isn't a libertarian distrust of government policy, which is healthy in any democracy. This is a deep skepticism about our society's institutions. And it's becoming more mainstream.

We can't trust the nightly news. We can't trust our politicians. Our universities, the gateway to a better life, are rigged against us. We can't get jobs. You can't believe these things and participate meaningfully in society. Social psychologists have shown that group belief is a powerful motivator of performance. When groups perceive that it's in their interest to work hard and achieve, members of that group outperform other similarly situated individuals. It's obvious why: If you believe that hard work pays off, you work hard; if you think it's hard to get ahead even if you try, why try at all?

Similarly, when people fail, this mindset allows them to look outward. I once ran into an old acquaintance in a Middletown bar who told me that he had recently quit his job because he was tired of waking up early. I later saw him on Facebook complaining about the "Obama economy" and how it had affected his life. I don't doubt that the Obama economy has affected many people, but this man is certainly not one of them. His status in life is directly attributable to the choices he's made, and his life will only improve if he makes better choices. But for him to make better choices, he needs to live in an environment that forces him to ask hard questions about himself. There is a cultural movement in the white working class to blame society or government for problems, and this movement is gaining adherents every day.

This is where the rhetoric of modern conservatives (and I say this as one of them) fails to meet the real challenges of their largest constituency. Instead of encouraging engagement, conservatives are increasingly fostering the kind of disengagement that has sapped the ambition of so many of my peers. I have watched some friends blossom into successful adults and others fall prey to the worst of Middletown's temptations - premature parenthood, drugs, incarceration. What separates the successful from the unsuccessful are the expectations they had for their own lives. Yet the message from the right is increasingly: It's not your fault you're a loser; it's the government's fault.

My father, for example, has never denigrated hard work, but he distrusts some of the most obvious paths to upward mobility. When he learned that I had decided to go to Yale Law, he asked if I had "pretended to be black or liberal" on my applications. This is how low the cultural expectations of white working-class Americans have fallen. We should not be surprised that as attitudes like these spread, the number of people willing to work for a better life declines.

The Pew Economic Mobility Project has studied how Americans view their chances for economic advancement, and what they found is shocking. No group of Americans is more pessimistic than working-class whites. Well over half of blacks, Latinos, and college-educated whites expect their children to be better off economically than they were. Among working-class whites, only 44 percent share this expectation. Even more surprising, 42 percent of working-class whites

- by far the highest number in the survey - say their lives are less economically successful than their parents'.

In 2010, that simply wasn't my mindset. I was happy where I was and overwhelmingly hopeful about the future. For the first time in my life, I felt like an outsider in Middletown. And what alienated me was my optimism.

Chapter 11

During my first round of law school applications, I didn't even apply to Yale, Harvard, or Stanford - the mythical "top three" schools. I didn't think I had a chance at those places. More importantly, I didn't think it mattered; all lawyers get good jobs, I assumed. All I had to do was get into any law school, and I'd be fine: a nice salary, a respectable profession, and the American dream. Then my best friend, Darrell, ran into one of his law school classmates at a popular restaurant in Washington. She was bussing tables because it was the only job available to her. Next round, I tried Yale and Harvard.

I didn't apply to Stanford - one of the best schools in the country - and to know why is to understand that the lessons I learned as a child were sometimes counterproductive. Stanford's law school application wasn't the standard combination of college transcript, LSAT score, and essays. It required a personal signature from the dean of your college: You had to submit a form filled out by the dean certifying that you weren't a loser.

I didn't know my college dean at Ohio State. It's a big place. I'm sure she's a lovely person, and the form was clearly little more than a formality. But I just couldn't ask. I had never met this person, never taken a class with her, and most importantly, I didn't trust her. Whatever virtues she possessed as a person, she was an outsider in the abstract. The professors I'd chosen to write my letters to had earned my trust. I listened to them almost every day, took their tests, and wrote papers for them. As much as I loved Ohio State and its people for an incredible education and experience, I couldn't put my fate in the hands of someone I didn't know. I tried to talk myself into it. I even printed the form and drove to campus. But when the time came, I crumpled it up and threw it in the trash. There would be no Stanford Law for J.D.

I decided I wanted to go to Yale more than any other school. It had an aura - with its small class sizes and unique grading system, Yale billed itself as a low-stress way to launch a legal career. But most of its students came from elite private colleges, not large state schools like mine, so I imagined I had no chance of getting in. Nevertheless, I applied online because it was relatively easy. It was late afternoon on an early spring day in 2010 when my phone rang and the caller ID showed an unfamiliar 203 area code. I answered, and the voice on the other line told me that it was the Director of Admissions at Yale Law, and that I had been admitted to the Class of 2013. I was ecstatic and jumped up and down for the entire three-minute conversation. By the time he said goodbye, I was so out of breath that when I called Aunt Wee to tell her, she thought I'd been in a car accident.

I was so committed to going to Yale Law that I was willing to accept the two hundred thousand dollars or so in debt I knew I'd be incurring. But the financial aid package Yale offered was beyond my wildest dreams. In my first year, it was almost a full ride. That wasn't because of anything I'd done or deserved-it was because I was one of the poorest kids in the school. Yale offered tens of thousands in need-based aid. It was the first time being so broke had ever paid off so well. Yale wasn't just my dream school, it was the cheapest option on the table.

The New York Times recently reported that the most expensive schools are, paradoxically, cheaper for low-income students. Take, for example, a student whose parents earn thirty thousand a year-not a lot of money, but not poverty level. That student would pay ten thousand at one of the University of Wisconsin's less selective branch campuses, but six thousand at the school's flagship campus in Madison. At Harvard, the student would pay only about thirteen hundred, despite a tuition of over forty thousand. Of course, kids like me don't know this. My buddy Nate, a lifelong friend and one of the smartest people I know, wanted to go to the University of Chicago as an undergraduate, but he didn't apply because he knew he couldn't afford it. It probably would have cost him considerably less than Ohio State, just as Yale cost me considerably less than any other school.

I spent the next few months getting ready to leave. My aunt and uncle's friend got me this job at a local floor tile distribution warehouse, and I worked there for the summer-driving a forklift, preparing shipments of tiles for transport, and sweeping a huge warehouse. By the end of the summer, I'd saved enough money not to worry about moving to New Haven.

The day I moved felt different than any other time I'd left Middletown. I knew when I left for the Marines that I'd be back often, and that life might bring me back to my hometown for extended periods of time (it did). After four years in the Marines, moving to Columbus for college didn't seem all that significant. I'd become an expert at leaving Middletown for other places, and each time I felt at least a little lost. But this time I knew I was never really coming back. That didn't bother me. Middletown no longer felt like home.

On my first day at Yale Law School, there were posters in the hallways announcing an event with Tony Blair, the former British Prime Minister. I couldn't believe it: Tony Blair was going to speak to a room of a few dozen students? Had he come to Ohio State, he would have filled an auditorium with a thousand people. "Yeah, he speaks at Yale all the time," a friend told me. "His son is a student." A few days later, I almost ran into a man as I turned a corner to enter the main entrance of the law school. I said, "Excuse me," looked up, and realized the man was New York Governor George Pataki. Things like that happen at least once a week. Yale Law School was like nerd Hollywood, and I never stopped feeling like an awestruck tourist.

The first semester was structured to make life easy for students. While my friends at other law schools were overwhelmed with work and worried about strict grading curves that effectively put you in direct competition with your classmates, our dean asked us during orientation to follow our passions wherever they might lead and not worry so much about grades. Our first four classes were graded on a credit/no-credit basis, which made that easy. One of those classes, a constitutional law seminar with sixteen students, became a kind of family for me. We called ourselves the Island of Misfit Toys because there was no real unifying force to our team-a conservative Appalachian hillbilly, the super-smart daughter of Indian immigrants, a black Canadian with decades of street smarts, a neuroscientist from Phoenix, an aspiring civil rights lawyer born a few minutes from Yale's campus, and an extremely progressive lesbian with a fantastic sense of humor, among others-but we became excellent friends.

That first year at Yale was overwhelming, but in a good way. I'd always been an American history buff, and some of the buildings on campus predate the Revolutionary War. Sometimes I'd walk around campus looking for the plaques that identified the age of the buildings. The buildings themselves were stunningly beautiful - towering masterpieces of Gothic Revival architecture. Inside, intricate stone carvings and wood paneling gave the law school an almost medieval feel. Sometimes you even hear we went to HLS (Hogwarts Law School). It's telling that the best way to describe the law school was with a reference to a series of fantasy novels.

The classes were hard and sometimes required late nights in the library, but they weren't that hard. Part of me thought I'd finally be exposed as an intellectual fraud, that the administration would realize they'd made a terrible mistake and send me back to Middletown with their sincerest apologies. Another part of me thought I could hack it, but only with extraordinary effort. After all, these were the brightest students in the world, and I didn't qualify. But in the end, it wasn't. Although there were rare geniuses walking the halls of the law school, most of my classmates were smart, but not intimidatingly so. In classroom discussions and on tests, I largely held my own.

Not everything was easy. I always considered myself a decent writer, but when I turned in a sloppy paper to a famously strict professor, he returned it with an extraordinarily critical comment. "Not good at all," he scribbled on one page. On another, he circled a large paragraph and wrote in the margin, "This is a pile of sentences masquerading as a paragraph. Fix it." I heard through the grapevine that this professor thought Yale should only accept students from places like Harvard, Yale, Stanford, and Princeton: "It's not our job to do remedial work, and too many of these other kids need it." That committed me to changing his mind. By the end of the semester, he called my writing "excellent" and admitted that he might have been wrong about public schools. As freshman year drew to a close, I felt triumphant-my professors and I got along well, I had earned solid grades, and I had a dream job for the summer-working for the chief counsel of a sitting U.S. senator.

Yet for all the joy and intrigue, Yale planted a seed of doubt in my mind about whether I belonged. This place was so beyond what I expected of myself. I knew zero Ivy League graduates back home; I was the first person in my nuclear family to go to college and the first person in my extended family to attend professional school. When I arrived in August 2010, Yale had educated two of the last three Supreme Court justices and two of the last six presidents, not to mention the sitting Secretary of State (Hillary Clinton). There was something bizarre about Yale's social rituals: the cocktail receptions and banquets that served as both professional networking and personal matchmaking events. I was living among the newly christened members of what people back home pejoratively call "the elite," and by all appearances, I was one of them: I am a tall, white, heterosexual male. I have never felt out of place in my life. But I did at Yale.

Part of that has to do with social class. A student survey found that over 95 percent of Yale Law students identified as upper-middle class or higher, and most of them identified as outright wealthy. Obviously, I was neither upper-middle class nor wealthy. Very few Yale Law School people are like me. They may look like me, but despite the Ivy League's obsession with diversity, virtually everyone-black, white, Jewish, Muslim, whatever-comes from intact families that never worry about money. Early in my freshman year, after a late night of drinking with my classmates, we all decided to stop at a chicken joint in New Haven. Our large group left a terrible mess: dirty plates, chicken bones, ranch dressing and soda splattered all over the tables, and so on. I couldn't imagine leaving it all for some poor guy to clean up, so I stayed behind. Out of a dozen classmates, only one person helped me: my buddy Jamil, who also came from a poorer background. Afterwards, I told Jamil that we were probably the only people in school who'd ever had to clean up someone else's mess. He just nodded his head in silent agreement.

Although my experience was unique, I never felt like a stranger in Middletown. Most people's parents had never been to college. My closest friends had all experienced some kind of domestic turmoil in their lives-divorces, remarriages, legal separations, or fathers who had spent time in prison. A few parents worked as lawyers, engineers, or teachers. They were "rich people" to Mamaw, but never so rich that I thought of them as fundamentally different. They still lived within walking distance of my house, sent their kids to the same high school, and generally did the same things as the rest of us. It never occurred to me that I didn't belong, even in the homes of some of my relatively wealthy friends.

At Yale Law School, I felt like my spaceship had crashed in Oz. People would say with a straight face that having a surgeon mother and an engineer father was middle class. In Middletown, $160,000 is an unimaginable salary; at Yale Law School, students expect to make that much in their first year out of law school. Many are already worried it will not be enough.

It wasn't just about the money or my relative lack of it. It was about people's perceptions. At Yale, for the first time in my life, I felt others viewed my life with intrigue. Professors and classmates seemed genuinely interested in what seemed to me a superficially boring story. I went to a mediocre public high school, my parents didn't go to college, and I grew up in Ohio. The same was true of almost everyone I knew. At Yale, none of these things were true of anyone. Even my service in the Marine Corps was fairly common in Ohio, but at Yale many of my friends had never spent time with a veteran of America's recent wars. In other words, I was an anomaly.

That's not necessarily a bad thing. For much of that first year of law school, I revelled in the fact that I was the only major Marine with a Southern twang at my elite law school. But as law school acquaintances became close friends, I became less comfortable with the lies I told about my own past. "My mother is a nurse," I told them. But of course that wasn't true. I didn't really know what my legal father - the one whose name was on my birth certificate - did for a living; he was a total stranger. No one except my best friends from Middletown, whom I asked to read my law school admissions essay, knew about the formative experiences that shaped my life. At Yale, I decided to change that.

I'm not sure what motivated that change. Part of it is that I stopped feeling ashamed: My parents' mistakes were not my fault, so I had no reason to hide them. But most of all, I was concerned that no one understood the outsized role my grandparents played in my life. Few of even my closest friends understood how utterly hopeless my life would have been without Mamaw and Papaw. So maybe I was just trying to give credit where credit is due.

But there's something else. As I realized how different I was from my classmates at Yale, I came to appreciate how similar I was to the people back home. Most importantly, I became acutely aware of the inner conflict created by my recent success. On one of my first visits home after classes began, I stopped at a gas station not far from Aunt Wee's house. The woman at the nearest pump struck up a conversation, and I noticed that she was wearing a Yale T-shirt. "Did you go to Yale?" I asked. "No," she replied, "but my nephew did. Did you?" I didn't know what to say. It was stupid-her nephew went there, for God's sake-but I still felt uncomfortable admitting that I'd become an Ivy Leaguer. The moment she told me that her nephew went to Yale, I had to make a choice: Was I a Yale law student or a Middletown kid with hillbilly grandparents? If the former, I could exchange pleasantries and talk about the beauty of New Haven; if the latter, she occupied the other side of an invisible divide and could not be trusted. At her cocktail parties and fancy dinners, she and her nephew probably even laughed at the unsophisticated people of Ohio and how they clung to their guns and religion. I would not associate with her. My response was a pathetic attempt at cultural defiance: "No,

I don't go to Yale. But my girlfriend is." And then I got in my car and left.

This wasn't one of my prouder moments, but it illustrates the inner conflict that rapid upward mobility inspires: I had lied to a stranger to avoid feeling like a traitor. There are lessons here, including what I've already noted: that one consequence of isolation is seeing standard measures of success as not only unattainable, but as the property of people not like us. Mamaw always fought this attitude in me, and she was mostly successful.

Another lesson is that it's not just our own communities that reinforce outsider attitudes, but the places and people that upward mobility connects us to - like my professor who suggested that Yale Law School should refuse applicants from non-prestigious state schools. There's no way to quantify how these attitudes affect the working class. What we do know is that working-class Americans are not only less likely to climb the economic ladder, they're also more likely to fall off once they get there. I imagine that the discomfort they feel in leaving behind much of their identity plays at least a small role in this problem. One way our upper class can promote upward mobility, then, is not only to push for smart public policies, but also to open their hearts and minds to the newcomers who don't quite fit in.

Although we sing the praises of social mobility, it has its downsides. The term necessarily implies some kind of movement-to a theoretically better life, yes, but also away from something. And you can't always control the parts of your old life you drift away from. In recent years I've vacationed in Panama and England. I've shopped at Whole Foods. I've gone to orchestra concerts. I've tried to kick my addiction to "refined processed sugars" (a term that contains at least one word too many). I've worried about racial bias in my own family and friends.

None of these things are bad. In fact, most of them are good - visiting England was a childhood dream; eating less sugar improves health. At the same time, they've shown me that social mobility isn't just about money and economics, it's about changing your lifestyle. The rich and powerful aren't just rich and powerful; they follow a different set of norms and mores. When you move from the working class to the professional class, almost everything about your old life becomes unfashionable at best, or unhealthy at worst. At no time was this more evident than the first (and last) time I took a Yale friend to Cracker Barrel. In my youth, it was the pinnacle of fine dining - my grandmother's and my favorite restaurant. With Yale friends, it was a greasy public health crisis.

These aren't huge problems, and if I had it to do over again, I'd trade a little social discomfort for the life I'm leading in a heartbeat. But as I realized that I was the cultural alien in this new world, I began to think seriously about questions that had been nagging at me since I was a teenager: Why did no one else from my high school make it into the Ivy League? Why are people like me so poorly represented in America's elite institutions? Why are domestic disputes so common in families like mine? Why did I think places like Yale and Harvard were so out of reach? Why did successful people feel so different from me?

Chapter 12

Usha, a classmate, became my crush as I contemplated my identity. Luckily, we were paired for our first large writing assignment, so we spent a lot of time together that first year. She appeared to be a genetic anomaly—smart, hardworking, tall, and gorgeous. I joked with a friend that she would have been a fantastic Ayn Rand heroine if she had a terrible personality, but she had a terrific sense of humor and spoke quite directly. Rather sheepishly asking, "Yes, perhaps you could rephrase that?" or "Have you thought about this other idea?" Usha said, "I think that statement needs revision," or "That's a bad argument. She observed to a mutual friend at a pub, without irony, "Your brain is small. I had never met anyone like her.

I dated other girls, seriously or not. But Usha was in another emotional world. My thoughts were always about her. One friend called me "heartbroken," and another said he had never seen me like this. I asked Usha after learning she was unmarried at the end of our freshman year. After weeks of flirting and one date, I confessed my love. It broke every modern dating norm I learned as a young guy, but I didn't care. Usha guided me through Yale. She knew the best coffee shops and restaurants from college. However, her expertise was deeper: she instantly grasped the questions I didn't know to ask and always encouraged me to seek out new options. "Go to office hours," she said. "Professors prefer talking to students. The experience includes it." Usha helped me feel at home in an unfamiliar place.

Yale educated me in law. I learned most from my first year at Yale that I didn't understand the world. Top law firm recruiters visit New Haven every August to find the next generation of legal talent. The Fall Interview Program (FIP) includes a week of dinners, cocktail hours, hospitality suite visits, and interviews for students. I received six interviews on my first day of FIP, before second-year courses, including one with Gibson Dunn, LLP, a top Washington, D.C. firm. The interview went nicely.

Gibson Dunn asked me to their legendary dinner at one of New Haven's most upscale restaurants after my interview went well. Rumor had it that the dinner was an interim interview: We had to be humorous, charming, and engaging or we wouldn't be asked to the D.C. or New York offices for the final interviews. I was disappointed to find my most costly meal in such a high-stakes setting when I arrived at the restaurant.

We were taken to a separate banquet area for wine and discussion before dinner. Women a decade older than me carried bottles of wine wrapped in exquisite linen and asked me every few minutes if I wanted a fresh glass or a refill. First, I was too anxious to drink. But I eventually had the confidence to answer yes when asked whether I wanted wine and what kind. "I'll have white," I said, hoping to resolve the issue. "Do you want sauvignon blanc or chardonnay?"

Thought she was pulling my leg. My deductions revealed it was two separate white wines. Because Chardonnay was easier to say, I ordered it instead of Sauvignon Blanc. I avoided my first gunshot. Yet the night was young.

These events require a balance between shyness and intimidation. Don't bother the partners, but don't let them leave without shaking your hand. I tried to be myself—I've always been social but not bossy. However, the atmosphere was so compelling that "being myself" meant gazing at the restaurant's nicer items and wondering how much they cost.

The wine glasses look like they've been Windexed. That dude did not buy his suit at the three-suits-for-one sale at Jos. A. Bank; it looks like it's made from silk. The linens on the table look softer than my bedsheets; I need to touch them without being weird about it. Long story short, I needed a new plan. By the time we sat down for dinner, I'd resolved to focus on the task at hand—getting a job—and leave the class for tourism later.

I waited two more minutes. After we sat down, the waiter asked if I wanted tap or sparkling water. As much as I liked the meal, calling the water "sparkling" was arrogant, like calling a diamond or crystal "sparkling". I requested sparkling water anyhow. Probably better for me. Fewer pollutants.

I just spat out a sip. It was the worst flavor I've had. When I had Diet Coke at Subway, the vending machine didn't have enough syrup. That upscale place's "sparkling" water tasted like that. "There's something wrong with this water," claimed. The waitress apologized and brought me another Pellegrino. Then I learned "sparkling" water meant "carbonated" water. Just one classmate saw, which was lucky. I felt horrified. I was clear. No more errors.

Soon later, I observed an unusual quantity of cutlery on the table. Nine utensils? Why did I need three spoons? Why so many butter knives? I remembered a movie scene and recognized there was a social norm for flatware placement and size. I called my spirit guide in the bathroom and asked, "What am I going to do with all these damn forks? I don't want to make a fool of myself." Usha's advice—"Go from outside to inside, and don't use the same utensil for different dishes; oh, and use the fat spoon for soup"—prepared me to impress my future employers at dinner.

The evening passed uneventfully. I spoke politely, remembering Lindsay's advice to chew with my mouth closed. Law, law school, firm culture, and politics were discussed around our table. We had wonderful recruiters, and everyone at my table got a job—even the guy who spit out his sparkling drink.

At that meal on the first of five exhausting days of interviews, I realized I was seeing the inner workings of a system most of my colleagues didn't know about. Our career office emphasizes sounding natural and being someone interviewers would like to sit with on a plane. It was obvious—who wants to work with an asshole? - but it seemed weird for a young career's most significant moment. Our Yale Law background gave us an advantage in interviews, so grades and resumes weren't as important. The interviews tested social skills including belonging, holding your own in a corporate boardroom, and connecting with new clients.

I didn't have to take the hardest test—getting an audience. I marveled at my easy access to the nation's top lawyers all week. All of my pals had at least 12 interviews, and most got jobs. After sixteen interviews, I was so spoiled (and fatigued) that I turned down a handful. Two years before, I had applied to dozens of places for a well-paying job after graduation but was rejected every time. After one year at Yale Law, men who had argued before the US Supreme Court offered my classmates and me six-figure sums.

I had connected with a mystery energy for the first time, and it was obvious. I always assumed you looked for jobs online in want of advertisements. Then you send 12 resumes. Then you hope someone calls back. You might get lucky and have a friend prioritize your resume. Field hunting may be easier if you're qualified for a high-demand field like accounting. Rules are mostly the same.

Almost everyone who follows those rules fails. I learned from this week's interviews that successful people play differently. They don't send out resumes in hopes of getting an interview. They link up. They email a friend of a friend to promote their name. Their uncles are college buddies. They schedule interviews months in advance with their school's career services office. Their parents told them how to dress, talk, and who to talk to.

That doesn't mean your resume or interview performance are irrelevant. Those things matter. However, economists regard social capital highly. It's a professorial term, but the idea is simple: Our social and institutional networks are economically valuable. They introduce us to people, create opportunities, and educate us. We're alone without them.

I discovered this the hard way during one of my last marathon FIP week interviews. Interviews were repetitive by now. They asked about my hobbies, favorite classes, and expected legal field. They asked if I had questions. My responses and queries were refined after 12 tries, making me sound like a law firm information consumer. It was true that I had no notion what I wanted to accomplish or what kind of law to practice. My questions about "firm culture" and "work-life balance" were unclear. The whole thing was a sham. I didn't seem like an asshole, so I coasted.

I hit a wall. The last interviewer asked me why I wanted to work for a law firm, which I couldn't answer. It was a softball, but I was so used to talking about my growing interest in antitrust lawsuits (which was partly contrived) that I was woefully unprepared. I should have mentioned learning from the best or high-stakes litigation. I should have responded with something other than "I don't really know, but the pay isn't bad! Ha ha!" The interviewer looked at me like I had three eyes, and the topic never recovered.

Was sure I was done. I blew the interview horribly. My reference was already answering phones backstage. She told the hiring partner I was a brilliant, good child who would make a great lawyer. "She raved about you," I learned. I qualified for the next round of interviews when the recruiters called. Even though I botched the most crucial phase of the hiring process, I got the job. The saying goes, "Luck is better than good." Apparently, the correct network beats both.

Networking power is like air at Yale—pervasive but easy to overlook. Most of us prepared for the Yale Law Journal essay competition in our first year. The Journal publishes lengthy legal analysis for academics. Dry, formulaic, and partially translated, the articles read like radiator instructions. "Despite the great promise of grading, we show that regulatory design, implementation, and practice suffer from serious flaws: jurisdictions fudge more than they nudge.") Journal membership is serious business. Some legal employers hire just from the publication's editorial board, making it their most important extracurricular.

Some law school students wanted to make the Yale Law Journal. Writing competition began in April. By March, some had prepared for weeks. A good friend started before Christmas on the advice of recent graduates and close friends. Elite consulting firm alumni debated editorial methods. A sophomore helped his old Harvard roommate (a freshman) plan studying for the final month before exams. People were using friendship circles and alumni networks to learn about our first year's most crucial test everywhere.

I had no idea what happened. No Ohio State alumni club existed—I was one of two Ohio State graduates in the law school. Since Justice Sonia Sotomayor was a member, I suspected the Journal was important. I didn't know why. I had no idea what the Journal does. Nobody I knew had the key to the black box process.

There were formal communication channels. But they sent contradictory messages. Yale is known for its low-stress, non-competitive law school. Unfortunately, this ethos can send mixed messages. It was unclear what the Journal was worth. We were advised that the Journal was a tremendous career boost, but not to worry about it, but that some jobs required it. For many vocations and hobbies, Journal membership was a waste of time. It wasn't clear which careers applied. I had no idea how to find out.

Amy Chua, one of my professors, explained how it worked: "Journal membership is useful if you want to work for a judge or be an academic. Otherwise, it's a waste. But if you're not sure what you want to do, go ahead and try." Million-dollar advice. As I wasn't sure what I wanted, I followed. In my second year, I became the editor of a prominent newspaper after failing my first. Whether I succeeded is irrelevant. The important thing is that a professor helped me fill the information gap. I felt like I could see.

Amy guided me again in uncharted land. Law school is a three-year life and career challenge. Having several possibilities is good. However, I had no notion what to do with those possibilities or which ones had long-term relevance. I had no long-term goal. Graduating and acquiring a good career was my goal. I thought about doing public service when I paid off my law school debt. But I had no career in mind.

Life wouldn't wait. Soon after I joined a legal firm, people started talking about clerkships after graduation. Judicial clerkships with federal judges last a year. Clerks read court papers, research legal issues for judges, and help them draft opinions, which is great training for young lawyers. Every former clerk marvels about the experience, and private-sector companies pay tens of thousands in signing bonuses.

That was my understanding of clerkships, and it was true. It was superficial; clerkship is far more complicated. First, select if you want to clerk for a trial court or an appeals court. Choose which regions of the country to apply to. Certain "feeder" judges improve your chances of clerking for the Supreme Court. As expected, feeder judges hire more competitively, thus hanging out for one risks losing a clerkship or reaching the nation's highest court. Consider that you will work closely with these judges. No one wants to squander a year being nagged by a black-robed jerk.

No database informs you which judges are friendly, which send individuals to the Supreme Court, and what kind of work you want to do—trial or appellate. It's nearly impolite to discuss these topics. How do you ask a professor if the judge he recommends is nice? It's harder than expected.

Your social network—student groups, clerked pals, and the rare professors who can give brutally honest advice—can provide this knowledge. I had learned at this point in law school that networking only works if you ask. So I did. Amy Chua advised me clerking for a prominent feeder judge wouldn't be advantageous for my goals. I persisted until she recommended me to a prominent federal judge with close links to many Supreme Court justices.

I sent a resume, polished writing sample, and frantic letter of interest. My motives were unknown. My Southern accent and lack of family history may have made me feel like I needed confirmation that I belonged at Yale Law. Maybe I followed the herd. Whatever the reason, I needed accreditation.

Amy phoned me into her office a few days after I submitted my documents to tell me I made the cut. My heart raced. I knew I'd get the job with an interview. I knew I'd get the interview if she pushed my application hard enough.

I discovered the value of actual social capital then. I'm not saying my professor called the judge to question me. Before she did, my lecturer said she wanted a serious conversation. She was sad: "I don't think you're doing this for the right reasons. I think you're doing it for the degree, which is fine, but the degree doesn't really serve your career goals. If you don't want to be a high-powered Supreme Court litigator, you shouldn't care so much about this job."

She said clerking with this judge would be difficult. His demands were high. His clerks worked nonstop for a year. She got personal. She knew my new girlfriend and my love for her. "This internship is the kind of thing that destroys relationships. If you want my advice, you should put Usha first and find a career that actually suits you."

I followed the best advice anyone had given me. I requested my application be withdrawn. Can't say if I'd have gotten the job. I certainly overestimated my grades and the résumé was good but not great. Amy's advice prevented me from making a life-changing choice. It prevented me from moving 1,000 miles from my future spouse. Most importantly, it helped me accept my role at this strange institution—it was alright to follow my own path and put a girl above any short-term ambition. My professor let me be myself. That advice is hard to value. It keeps paying off. However, that advice was economically valuable. Social capital goes beyond connecting you with a friend or sending a CV to an old boss. How much we learn from friends, coworkers, and mentors is also, or mostly, measured. I had no idea how to prioritize my alternatives or that there were better ones. I learned these from my network, especially a helpful educator. My social capital education continues. I once contributed to The Atlantic's journalist and thought leader David Frum's website. When I was ready to commit to a Washington law firm, he suggested another where two Bush administration friends had become senior partners. One friend interviewed me and mentored me when I joined his firm. This man introduced me to Indiana Governor Mitch Daniels, my political hero and Bush White House friend, at a Yale conference. I would never have worked at that firm or chatted briefly with my favorite public figure without David's counsel. I wanted to be a clerk. Instead of going in blind, I understood what I wanted: to work for someone I admired, learn as much as I could, and be near Usha. Usha and I decided to clerk together. We relocated to Northern Kentucky, near my hometown. Best possible situation. We invited our clerkship supervisors to officiate our wedding since we liked them.

One view of successful people's lives. But social capital is everywhere. Those who apply it succeed. Those without a major handicap in life. This is a major issue for kids like myself. Here's a partial list of things I didn't know at Yale Law School:

That you needed to wear a suit to a job interview.
Wearing a suit large enough to fit a silverback gorilla was inappropriate.
That a butter knife wasn't just decorative (after all, anything that requires a butter knife can be done better with a spoon or an index finger).
That pleather and leather were different substances.
That your shoes and belt should match.
That certain cities and states had better job prospects.
That going to a nicer college brought benefits outside of bragging rights.
That finance was an industry that people worked in.

Mamaw always hated the hillbilly stereotype of drooling idiots. I was quite uninformed about success. Not knowing what others know can hurt the economy. It cost me a job in college (apparently Marine Corps combat boots and khaki slacks are not interview clothing) and may have cost me more in law school if I hadn't gotten some aid.

Chapter 13

Beginning my second year of law school, I felt accomplished. I returned to New Haven with new acquaintances and experiences after a summer at the Senate. My wonderful girlfriend and good legal job were almost there. Since kids like me weren't supposed to succeed, I was proud. I outperformed Mom's addiction and Dad's abandonment. Mamaw and Papaw weren't there, my biggest regret.

However, my relationship with Usha showed signs of difficulty. A few months into dating, she presented an analogy that fit me perfectly. She called me turtle. "When something terrible happens—even a slight disagreement—you withdraw completely. A shell for hiding."

It was true. Because I couldn't handle interpersonal situations, I ignored them. It seemed terrible to scold her if she did something wrong. I can withdraw. No more arrows in my quiver. I thought my family didn't pass on worry, despair, fear, and anxiety, but fighting it did. It was intense and complete.

Usha blocked my exit. After several tries, she said quitting everything was silly unless I didn't care about her. Screamed. I'd commit my mother's crimes. I'd feel guilty and scared. I'd villainized Mom for years. Now I acted like her. The fear of becoming your closet monster is unsurpassed.

Usha and I went to D.C. for follow-up legal firm interviews in our second year of law school. I returned to our hotel room unhappy after failing at a company I wanted to work for. Usha comforted me by stating I probably did better than planned, but there were other fish in the sea. I raged. "Don't tell me I did well," I yelled. You rationalize weakness. Making excuses for failure didn't get me here."

After leaving the hotel, I went around DC's commercial district for hours. After a shouting match with Bob, Mom took me and our toy poodle to the Comfort Inn in Middletown. We spent a few days there before Mamaw advised Mom to go home and deal with her troubles. Mom, her mother, and sister fled out the back door to avoid another night of terror with her drunken father as children. I fled third-generation.

Nearby was Ford's Theatre, where Booth shot Lincoln. A small store half a block from the theater sells Lincoln memorabilia. A gigantic Lincoln doll with a wide grin watches visitors inside. I felt this inflatable Lincoln was mocking me. The hell is he happy? Personal thoughts. Lincoln was depressed, so a stone's throw from his headshot wouldn't make him smile.

I turned the corner to find Usha on Ford's Theatre stairs. She chased me, worried I was alone. I realized I had to figure out why my family had mistreated people for decades. Many apologies to Usha. I expected her to tell me to screw myself, that my blunders would take days to repair, and that I was terrible. A sincere apology is a surrender, and surrenderers are attacked. Usha was uninterested. She calmly told me through tears that running away was never acceptable, that she was terrified, and that I needed to learn how to talk to her. She hugged me and said she understood my apology and was glad I was okay. That ended.

Usha learned to fight without hillbilly training. The lack of drama when I visited her family for Thanksgiving surprised me. Mother didn't criticize Usha's dad secretly. No family friends were accused of lying or betraying, and no wife-sister disputes occurred. Usha's parents loved her grandma and siblings. I anticipated a character assault when I asked her father about a distant cousin. I heard compassion, sadness, and a life lesson: "I still call for him. Uninterested relatives can't be ignored. Try because they're family.

I tried counseling but found it bizarre. Sharing my feelings with a stranger made me uncomfortable. The library demonstrated that my supposed common conduct was studied rigorously. Psychologists call my and Lindsay's daily encounters "adverse childhood experiences," or ACEs. Adults experience childhood traumas (ACEs). Trauma need not be physical. ACEs involve these feelings or events:

•being sworn at, insulted, or humiliated by parents

•being pushed, grabbed, or having something thrown at you
•feeling that your family didn't support each other
•having parents who were separated or divorced
•living with an alcoholic or a drug user
•living with someone who was depressed or attempted suicide
•watching a loved one be physically abused.

Every community has ACEs. However, research shows that my population has greater ACEs. Less than half of college-educated non-workers had ACEs, according to the Wisconsin Children's Trust Fund. Over half of working-class adults had ACEs, and 40% had numerous. This is shocking—four out of ten working class people endured multiple childhood traumas. Non Workers: 29%.

Aunt Wee, Uncle Dan, Lindsay, and Usha took a psychologist-designed ACEs quiz. Lindsay and I scored six, but Aunt Wee scored seven. Dan and Usha, from weirdly kind families, scored zero. Childhood trauma-free people were weird.

ACE-rich kids are more likely to suffer anxiety, depression, heart disease, obesity, and cancer. School underperformance and insecure adult relationships are also common. Extra weeping might undermine a child's security and cause mental health and behavioral disorders later in life.

Harvard pediatricians studied childhood trauma's mental effects. According to specialists, chronic stress can damage a child's brain chemistry and lead to health issues. Physiological stress. Adrenaline and other hormones rush our system when stimulated. Fight-or-flight is taught in elementary school. It may inspire ordinary folks to be brave. It's how mothers can carry heavy objects with their children underneath and how an unarmed elderly woman can fight a mountain lion to save her husband.

Fight-or-flight is harmful and persistent. Great solution, says Dr. Nadine Burke Harris. If a bear is in the woods. That bear coming home from the bar every night is the problem." Harvard researchers revealed the high-stress brain dominates. "Significant stress in early childhood," they add, "results in a hyperreactive or chronically activated physiological stress response, along with an increased potential for fear and anxiety." For kids like myself, the stress and conflict center is always on. We are constantly exposed to the bear, whether it is an alcoholic father or an unstable mother, so we can fight or escape. We fight often. That wiring lasts after war.

It transcends battling. American working-class households are more unstable overall. Examine moms' father-figure rotation. Another country has nothing like it. 0.5 percent of French children have three or more mothers. The second-highest number is 2.6 percent in Sweden, 1 in 40. It's 8.2% in the US, or one in twelve, and much higher among the working class. The worst part is that interpersonal instability, like household upheaval, cycles. According to sociologists Paula Fornby and Andrew Cherlin, "Multiple family structure shifts may harm children's development.

Many youngsters automatically flee, but rarely choose the right door. My aunt married an abusive man at sixteen. My high school salutatorian mother had a baby, divorce, and no college credits before her teens. Frying pan to fire. The chaos breeds chaos. Instability breeds. American hillbilly family life.

Knowing my past and that I wasn't doomed gave me hope and strength to overcome my teenage troubles. Though clichéd, chatting to people who understood was best. Aunt Wee instinctively claimed we had similar relationships: "Yes. She said I was always ready to fight Dan..." "Sometimes I'd even prepare for a big fight - like physically putting myself in a fighting position - before he stopped talking." Shocked. Aunt Wee and Dan have the best marriage. They act like they just started dating after 20 years. Her marriage improved after she stopped being defensive.

Lindsay verified. "When I fought Kevin, I insulted him and ordered him to leave, which he would. Like, 'What's wrong?' Why are you fighting me like the enemy? Indeed, our home made it hard to tell friends from antagonists. Lindsay is still married 16 years.

Eighteen years at home made me think about myself and my emotional triggers. Apologies were used to relax, thus I distrusted them. My "I'm sorry" drove me on that disastrous road trip with Mom over a decade before. I recognized I and everyone else used words as weapons to survive. You played to win in war.

Lessons were not forgotten overnight. With sometimes-stacked statistics, I struggle with confrontation. Sometimes knowing the statistics say I should be in prison or fathering my fourth illegitimate child helps. Conflict and family disintegration appear inevitable, making it hard. In my worst moments, I believe to myself there is no way out and that past demons are my heritage, like my blue eyes and brown hair, no matter how hard I try. Unfortunately, I needed Usha. My best self is a delayed explosion that requires precision to defuse. Usha also dominates me. Two men in a house are radioactive. My Aunt Wee, Lindsay, and cousin Gail—all wealthy homebuilders— married outside our culture.

Knowing this ruined my life. I thought I was better. Was strong. I left the city, joined the Marines, scored well at Ohio State, and got into the best legal school. Devils, character flaws, and difficulties were absent. It wasn't. I needed constant mental focus to attain my biggest goals— a happy partner and home. Self-image was bitterness disguised as arrogance. A few weeks into my second year of law school, I hadn't spoken to Mom in months, longer than ever. Despite my love, sympathy, forgiveness, fury, hatred, and dozens of others, I realized I had never tried to feel compassion for my mother. Never tried to understand my mother. At my most empathetic, I prayed I hadn't inherited her terrible genetic flaw. As I resembled Mom, I tried to understand her.

Uncle Jimmy had heard Mamaw and Papaw chatting years ago. Mom had issues and needed help. Bailouts were common and always had theoretical prerequisites. She'd be told to budget and given an arbitrary plan. Strategy cost her aid. Papaw sobbed while talking, which Uncle Jimmy had never seen him do. "I failed them," he cried. I failed her, my girl, he repeated.

Papa's strange breakdown begs a crucial question for hillbillies like me: How much of our good and bad lives are down to personal choices and society, families, and parents who failed their children? Mom's life—how much is her fault? Beginning and end of compassion and blame?

Everyone has views. Dad's responsibility for Mom's choices angers Uncle Jimmy. "Stayed with her. It was her fault. Aunt Wee agrees— who can blame her? At nineteen months younger than Mom, she saw Mamaw and Papaw at their worst and made her own mistakes before surviving. Mom should do it if she can. Lindsay is more sympathetic, thinking Mom's life gave her demons like ours. Lindsay advises taking responsibility and apologizing.

My take is mixed. Whatever my mother's parents' role in my life, their constant fighting and alcoholism must have hurt. My aunt and mother reacted differently to conflicts as youngsters. Aunt Wee would beg her parents to calm down or encourage her father to cool her mother while Mom would hide, run away, or collapse on the floor with her hands over her ears. She handled it worse than her siblings. Mom is like Vance's statistic-losing child. Maybe my family is lucky only one lost that game.

Mom isn't evil, I know. She loves Lindsay and me. She worked hard for motherwell. Sometimes she won, sometimes lost. She sought satisfaction in love and profession, but she often heard the wrong voice. Mom is mostly to blame. Lindsay, Aunt Wee, Mom, and I don't get childhood moral parole.

Nobody, not even Mamaw, could arouse my emotions like my mother. I smacked a kindergartener in the face for mocking her umbrella because I loved her. As she fell into addiction again and again, I hated her and wished she would take enough narcotics to abandon me and Lindsay forever. I felt rage that might have killed her as she screamed in bed after another failed relationship.

Lindsay called me at the end of law school to tell Mom was hooked on heroin and trying recovery again. I didn't know Mom's rehab background or how many nights she spent in the hospital barely awake due to drugs. So I shouldn't have been surprised or scared, since "heroin" sounds like the drug Derby. Mom's latest chemical choice haunted me for weeks. Maybe I'd given up on her.

Mom instilled fear, not love or hatred. Her safety concerns. Fear Lindsay would relive Mom's troubles while I was hundreds of miles away. My greatest fear was not escaping. Months before Yale Law graduation, I should have felt wonderful. I questioned if people like us can change, as I did much of the year.

My cousins Denise and Gail, Mamaw's brothers David and Pet's daughters, witnessed Usha and me graduate with 18 others. Also came were Usha's parents and uncle, wonderful people but quieter than our crew. When her family met mine, we behaved. (Denise criticized the museum's modern "art"!) Mom's addiction ended in a sad truce. Since she wasn't using it, I didn't mind her missing my graduation. At graduation, Justice Sonya Sotomayor said it was acceptable to be uncertain about our future. She presumably meant our careers, but I carried it farther. My Yale law education was substantial. However, I learned that this new environment will always feel foreign to me and that hillbillies commonly confused love and strife. That was my biggest graduation concern.

Chapter 14

I remember the filthy spiders best. Large ones, like tarantulas. A woman (who didn't major in hospitality management) was across the thick glass from me at a dismal roadside motel window. Her office light illuminated a few cobwebs between the structure and the makeshift sunscreen, which seemed ready to collapse. Every web had at least one large spider, and I imagined one would jump on my face and suck my blood if I looked away too long. I'm not terrified of spiders, but these were huge.

Not meant to be here. My life was designed to avoid places like these. I wanted to leave my hometown, "getting out," from this kind of environment. It was past midnight. The streetlight showed a man partly inside his truck, his feet dangling over to the side, and a hypodermic needle protruding from his arm. I should have been astonished, but this was Middletown. A few weeks previously, authorities found a woman passed out in the car wash with a bag of heroin and a spoon on the passenger seat and the needle still in her arm.

The hotel manager that night was the saddest. Even though she was forty, her long, gray, greasy hair, toothless mouth, and millstone frown spoke of old age. That woman had a terrible life. Her voice is like an infant's. The sound sounded faint and sorrowful.

She was unprepared when I gave her my credit card. "People usually pay cash," she said. I assured her, "I'll use a credit card, as I mentioned over the phone. I can rush to an ATM for you." I forgot, sorry. But that's okay—we have one around here." She grabbed an outdated card swipe machine that prints card information on yellow paper. When I gave her the card, her eyes begged, as if she were a prisoner in her own life. She said, "Enjoy your stay," which seemed odd. I had told her by phone less than an hour ago that the room was for my homeless mother. "Okay," I said. "Thank you."

I was a recent Yale Law School graduate, former Yale Law Journal editor, and lawyer in good standing. Two months ago, Usha and I were married in eastern Kentucky on a gorgeous day. My entire family attended, and we both changed our names to Vance, giving me the same name as my family. I loved Cincinnati, had a nice career, a new home, a lovely relationship, and a happy existence. After law school, Usha and I lived there with our two dogs for a year on an internship. I rose. I succeeded. I fulfilled the American dream.

From the outside, it looked that way. However, upward mobility is never pure, and the world I left continually draws me back. I don't remember how I got to the hotel, but I recognized the key points. Mom resumed using. Her fifth husband kicked her out after she stole family heirlooms to buy narcotics (prescribed opiates, I suppose). She had nowhere to go after their divorce.

I swore I'd never help Mom again, but I changed. I was uncomfortable exploring the Christian faith I'd abandoned years earlier. For the first time, I understood Mom's childhood emotional wounds. I realized that scars never healed, even for me. When Mom got in trouble, I didn't mumble abuses and hung up. I offered aid.

I tried calling a Middletown motel to give them my credit card. I thought $150 a week would give us time to plan. I drove from Cincinnati to Middletown (approximately an hour each way) around 11 p.m. on a Tuesday night to save Mom from being homeless because they wouldn't take my card over the phone.

My plan looked straightforward. I'd give Mom enough money to recover. Finding her own place, saving money to obtain her nursing license again, and going from there. To keep her fiscally clean, I'd watch her accounts. I remembered Mamaw and Papaw "plans" but vowed to do it differently.

It was easy to help Mom. My past was reconciled and a difficulty from elementary school was solved. I could calmly help Mom overcome her addiction because I had sympathy and understood her childhood. But dealing with that dirty accommodation was hard. And managing her finances as I desired required more patience and time than I had.

Thank God, I'm no longer hiding from Mom. I can't cure everything. Now there is a place for fury at Mom for her life and compassion for her lost childhood. I can help Mom when funds and emotions allow. But I also recognize my limitations and am willing to remove myself from Mom when it means too little money to pay my bills or too little patience for my loved ones. The shaky peace I've established with myself is working for now.

I'm sometimes asked if we can "solve" my community's problems. I know what they want: a miraculous policy or innovative government initiative. Not like a Rubik's Cube, these family, faith, and culture issues don't have answers (as most people understand them). A close buddy who served in the White House and cares for the working class told me, "Realize you probably can't solve these things. They're always present. But maybe you can weigh in for the marginalized."

Many thumbs on my scale. My life is marked by how many factors had to align to give me a shot. My grandparents were always there, even after my mother and stepfather moved far away to avoid them. Despite the constant turnover of parent figures, kind guys surrounded me. My mother inspired a lifetime passion of study despite her flaws. Though I outgrew her, my sister always protected me. Dan and Aunt Wee welcomed me when I was too terrified to ask. I saw my first wonderful, loving marriage long before that. There were teachers, distant relatives, and friends.

If any of those people leave, I'm probably screwed. Others who beat the odds describe similar interventions. Appalachian State University transfer student office manager Jane Rex. She was the first in her working-class family to attend college. After over forty years of marriage, she has three successful children. When asked what changed her life, she'll say her solid family empowered her and gave her choice over her destiny. She'll explain how traveling the globe may inspire enormous dreams: "You need solid role models. I got to witness different things because one of my best friends' father was the bank president. I knew there was another life, because exposure gives you dreams.

My cousin Gail, one of my mother's first Blanton grandchildren, is one of my favorites. Gail has a gorgeous home, three great kids, a loving marriage, and a saintly demeanor—the American Dream. Except for Mamaw Blanton, who we grandkids and great-grandchildren revere, no one has been dubbed "the kindest person in the world. Gail deserves the title.

I thought Gail's fairytale life came from her parents. I didn't think anyone was that polite, especially someone who'd suffered. However, Gail was a Blanton and a hillbilly, and I should have understood that every hillbilly makes it to maturity with a few huge mistakes. Home life brought Gail emotional baggage. When her father left, she was seven and graduated high school at seventeen, planning to attend the University of Miami. However, "Mom said I couldn't go to college without breaking up with my boyfriend. I moved away the day after graduation and was pregnant by August."

Her life unraveled quickly. When she welcomed a black child, racism surfaced. After announcements and fights, Gail lost her family. "I hadn't heard from any of our relatives," Gail said. "My mother said she never wanted to hear my name again."

Her marriage ended quickly due to her age and lack of family support. Gail had lost her family and gained a little kid who depended on her, complicating her life. Being a mother transformed my life—it defined me. Hippie or not, I had rules—no drugs, alcohol, or anything that might get social services to take my baby."

Gail: adolescent single mom, no family, little support. Many would have wilted, but the hillbilly won. "Dad wasn't around for years," Gail says, "so I didn't talk to Mom. But I recall one thing they taught me: we could do anything. I wanted this baby and its success. So I did." She rose at a local phone firm and returned to college. By the time she remarried, she was rolling. Her fairytale marriage to Allan, her second husband, is the cherry on top. In my hometown, Gail's story often resurfaces. You see teens in trouble, sometimes their own. Many fall victim to crime, early death, domestic trouble, and welfare dependency due to the odds. Others succeed. There's Jane Rex.

Lindsay grew up following Mamaw's death, and Aunt Wee turned her life around after leaving an abusive spouse. They all gained from similar experiences. They had a reliable relative. They learned from a family friend, uncle, or work mentor what was possible.

A team of economists, including Raj Chetty, produced a seminal study on opportunity in America shortly after I began thinking about how to help the American working class. They concluded that impoverished kids have fewer chances of succeeding in America's meritocracy than most of us would want. They thought many European countries were better at the American Dream than America. More crucially, they found that opportunity was unevenly distributed throughout. Utah, Oklahoma, and Massachusetts were thriving on the American Dream, better than anywhere else. Poor youth struggled in the South, Rust Belt, and Appalachia. Many were startled by their findings, but not me. Not anyone who'd been there. Chetty and his co-authors found that income segregation and single-parent households explained the uneven spatial distribution of opportunity in a paper. Growing up with many single mothers and fathers and living in an impoverished neighborhood limits your opportunities. It means that without Mamaw and Papaw to keep you going, you may never escape. You don't have people to demonstrate the benefits of hard effort and education. It means everything that made me, Lindsay, Gail, Jane Rex, and Aunt Wee happy is gone. I wasn't shocked that Mormon Utah, with its strong church, cohesive neighborhoods, and intact families, devastated Rust Belt Ohio.

My life may teach us how to put our thumb on the scale in policy. We can change how social services treat families like mine. I witnessed my mother dragged away in a police van when I was twelve. I'd seen her arrested before, but this was different. We had social worker visits and mandatory family counseling. A court date hanging like a guillotine. The caseworkers were supposed to protect me, but they became roadblocks early on. When I told them I spent most of my time with my grandparents and wanted to continue, they said the courts wouldn't accept it. Legally, my grandmother was an inexperienced, unlicensed caregiver. If my mother lost in court, I was as likely to end up in foster care as Mamaw. Being apart from everyone and everything I loved was terrifying. Thus, I kept quiet, assured the social workers everything was alright, and hoped to keep my family after the court hearing.

Mom avoided incarceration, and I stayed with Mamaw. If I didn't want to stay with Mom, Mamaw's door was always open. Mamaw would kill anyone who tried to separate us. Mamaw was insane and our family feared her, so this worked. Not everyone can rely on a crazy hillbilly. If they fall through, many youngsters have nothing left but children's services.

State definitions of family contribute to the issue. My family, like many black and Hispanic families, relies heavily on grandparents, cousins, aunts, and uncles. Like in my case, child welfare agencies excluded them. Some states require foster parents to be licensed like nurses and doctors, even if they are grandmothers or other close relatives. In other words, our social services weren't designed for rural households and often worsened problems.

I wish things were easy, but it's not. Foster children, mostly underprivileged, number 640,000 per year. Add the unknown number of abused or neglected children who flee foster care, and you have an epidemic that present policies are worsening.

There are alternative options. Understanding what hinders youngsters like me can help us design legislation. My biggest life lesson isn't that society didn't give me chances. My elementary and middle schools were fine, with teachers that tried to reach me. It was the students, not the staff, that put our high school toward the bottom of Ohio. Pell Grants, government-subsidized, low-interest student loans, and need-based law school scholarships make college cheap. I never went hungry because of Mamaw's hefty retirement benefits. These programs are imperfect, but I nearly made my worst choices (and I got close), and the blame is almost completely on variables outside the government's control.

My Middletown High professors and I met recently. All expressed concern that society is allocating too many resources too late. "It's like our politicians think college is the only way," a teacher said. It's fantastic for many. Many of our kids won't graduate from college." Another said: "They've only witnessed violence and fighting since childhood. My student misplaced her baby like her car keys—no idea where she went. Two weeks later, the child arrived in New York City with her drug dealer father and family. We all know that unfortunate baby's fate unless a miracle occurs. There's little support for her now, when intervention would assist. I think any successful policy program would recognize what my old high school teachers observe every day: that home life is the true issue for so many of these kids. We recognize that Section 8 vouchers shouldn't isolate the impoverished into little communities. Middletown instructor Brian Campbell said, "A huge base of Section 8 parents and children supported by fewer middle-class taxpayers is an upside-down triangle. A neighborhood with exclusively low-income residents has fewer emotional and financial resources. You can't combine them because it increases despondency. Yet, he continued, "when you put the low-income kids with those who have a different lifestyle model, the low-income kids start to rise." The federal government objected when Middletown tried to limit Section 8 vouchers in some neighborhoods. Perhaps keeping those kids from the middle class is best. Government policies may not solve other community issues. As a child, I linked academic success to femininity. Males were strong, brave, willing to battle, and successful with girls. Boys with good grades were "sissies" or "faggots. I have no idea where the feeling came from. No, not from Mamaw, who required good marks, or Papaw. But it was there, and studies show that working-class lads like me do poorly in school because they view homework as feminine. Can new laws or programs change that? Probably not. Not all scales are thumb-friendly.

I've discovered that my childhood survival traits hinder my adult achievement. Conflict makes me flee or prepare for a fight. This is pointless in my current relationships, but my childhood homes would have engulfed me without it. Young me learned to scatter my money around so Mom or someone else could "borrow" it—under the mattress, in the underwear drawer, at Mom's house. Usha was surprised when we merged our money and found that I had various bank accounts and little credit card balances. Usha still reminds me that not every imagined slight—from a passing vehicle or a neighbor criticizing my dogs—is a blood feud. Despite my intense emotions, I always realize she's probably right. Someone cut me off in Cincinnati a few years ago while driving with Usha. After honking my horn, the guy cut me off, and we stopped at a red light with him in front of me. I unbuckled my seat belt and opened the car door. I wanted to demand an apology and attack the guy, but was smart and locked the door before stepping out of the car. Usha was glad I changed my mind before she yelled at me to stop acting like a madman (which she has done before) and told me she was proud of me for resisting my impulse. The other driver insulted my honor, which kept the school bully from bothering me, connected me to my mother when a man or his children insulted her (even if I agreed with the insult), and gave me something, however small, over which I had complete control. Backing down earned me a "pussy" or "wimp" or "girl" reprimand for the first eighteen years of my life. Most of my life taught me that an upstanding young man hated the objectively proper course of action. A few hours after doing the right thing, I silently scolded myself. That's progress, right? Better than jail time for teaching that guy defensive driving.

Printed in Dunstable, United Kingdom